Balancing
the books

Micah and Nahum simply explained

Michael Bentley

EP BOOKS

(Evangelical Press) Unit C, Tomlinson Road, Leyland, England, PR25 2DY

www.epbooks.org
epbooks@10ofthose.com

First Published 1994
This edition 2015

Unless otherwise indicated, Scripture quotations in this publication are from the Holy Bible, New International Version. Copyright © 1973, 1978, 1984 International Bible Society. Published by Hodder & Stoughton.

British Library Cataloguing in Publication Data

ISBN 978-0-85234-324-1

To my dear friends of
Lipasmata Free Evangelical Church, Pireaus, Greece;
and to Brother Spyros Portinos and Sister Jennifer Jack, who are
faithful servants of the Lord in that church—and beyond

Contents

5

Preface

'I'm so glad that we're back in the New Testament again.' This is what one of our young men said to me the week after I had finished preaching the series of sermons upon which this book is based. I assume that he still had that 'sixth-form mentality' which believes that the God of the Old Testament and the God of the New Testament are different from each other—the first fierce and full of judgement, and the second exclusively loving and gracious. But what a travesty that thinking makes of the Lord God Almighty! The God of the Old Testament and the God of the New Testament are one and the same, and the Bible is a unity, not two distinct revelations. Because God is one, judgement and mercy, punishment and grace, and wrath and love are found throughout the whole Bible. Just as die Lord Jesus Christ speaks about the punishment of unrepentant sinners in hell, so the Old Testament declares God to be one who washes away all the iniquities of those who confess their sin and seek forgiveness in him (Psalm 51:2, 7).

One day, many years ago, I remember standing on a busy pavement in London pouring out my heart to a godly friend of mine because of the immoral behaviour of someone who was close to me. With tears in his eyes he looked straight at me and said, in a very quiet and lovely way,

> Who is a pardoning God like thee?
> Or who has grace so rich and free?"[1]

These words based on Micah 7:18 have often been a great comfort to me since that time, as they have been to very many others down through the centuries.

As I preached through these two prophetic books during the autumn of 1992, we were all often challenged by the realization that God is just and one day he will balance the books and all, without exception, will have to give an account of themselves.

The messages of Micah and Nahum were applied to our church at that time in numerous ways—not least as we saw several families decide that our church was not the one for them. The result was that the size of our congregation was somewhat smaller at the end of the series than it was when I started to preach through these prophetic books. Nevertheless we discovered that God did shepherd us with his staff, and we were the flock of his inheritance (see Micah 7:14). We became aware that the Lord was in control of events in our church, in the locality and nationally, and we perceived that 'There on the mountains [was] the feet of one who brings good news, who proclaims peace' (Nahum 1:15).

It is my desire that those who read this little book will be directed to the Lord—the one who brings 'the peace of God, which transcends all understanding'—and that he will guard each heart and mind in Christ Jesus (Philippians 4:7).

Michael Bentley
Bracknell
September 1994

Introduction to Micah and Nahum

Although both of these servants of God prophesied to the people of the southern kingdom of Judah, Nahum delivered his messages about one hundred years later than Micah. However, despite the distance in time between these two prophets, there are many common themes in these books, and one in particular—the powerful nation of Assyria.

The presence of Assyria was an awesome threat which loomed over Judah for the best part of one hundred years—between 736 BC and 836 BC. For many centuries before this Assyria had been growing in strength, but from about 736 BC the kings of Assyria began to have ambitions to expand their kingdom by absorbing the nations which surrounded their territory.

There are many documented proofs of the wickedness of this people; they inflicted very severe tortures on the prisoners whom they took and they breathed fear into the inhabitants of all of the neighbouring lands.

Assyria took away captive many of the inhabitants of Judah's northern neighbour, Israel, and Isaiah prophesied in the light of God's judgement upon them. He 'knew that the social and political collapse of the northern kingdom had been caused by its failure to pay due attention to the demands of the law from Mt Sinai. And he could see the same thing happening in Judah.'[1] Both Isaiah and Micah denounced the unfair treatment of the poor by the rich; they were horrified at the flouting of God's laws by those who should have known better. But Micah felt the smart even more than his contemporary because, unlike Isaiah, he was a prophet of the common people and country life. 'No class was free from corrupting influences; princes, priests, and people alike were all affected (Micah 2:2, 8–9, 11; 3:1–3, 5, 11) ... Micah wanted the people to know that every cruel act to one's fellow man was an insult to God.'[2]

Micah

The book of Micah falls naturally into three parts, each one beginning with the expression, 'Hear' or 'Listen' (1:2; 3:1; 6:1). At the end of each of these sections there is a message of hope. At the end of the first part we read,

> 'I will surely gather all of you, O Jacob;
> I will surely bring together the remnant of Israel.
> I will bring them together like sheep in a pen,
> like a flock in its pasture;
> the place will throng with people.
> One who breaks open the way will go up before them;
> they will break through the gate and go out.
> Their king will pass through before them,
> the Lord at their head'   (Micah 2:12–13).

At the end of the second section we read,

> 'The remnant of Jacob will be
> in the midst of many peoples
> like dew from the Lord,
> like showers on the grass,

which do not wait for man
or linger for mankind' (Micah 5:7).

The passage continues to speak of this remnant being like a lion which will enable God's people to be lifted up in triumph over their enemies (Micah 5:8-15).

Finally, at the completion of the third passage we read that Judah is told of the God 'who pardons sin and forgives the transgression of the remnant of his inheritance' (Micah 7:18). The prophet goes on to inform the people that their gracious God will not stay angry for ever but he will delight to show mercy:

'You will again have compassion on us;
you will tread our sins underfoot
and hurl all our iniquities into the depths of the sea.
You will be true to Jacob,
and show mercy to Abraham,
as you pledged on oath to our fathers
in the days long ago' (Micah 7:18-20).

In the midst of the alternating themes of gloom and triumph Micah lists many of the national sins of Judah. These are idolatry (1:7; 6:16), covetousness (2:2), oppression (2:2), violence (2:2; 3:10; 6:12; 7:2), encouraging false prophets (2:6, 11), corruption of princes (3:1-3), corruption of prophets (3:5-7), corruption of priests (3:11), bribery (3:9, 11; 7:3) and dishonesty (6:10-11).

However, there are also passages which speak clearly of the coming Messiah. One of the most well-known verses in Micah names his birthplace (5:2). The Messiah is displayed as King (2:12-13) and he is described as reigning in righteousness over the whole earth (4:1, 7).

Three times this prophecy is quoted elsewhere in the Bible. In

Jeremiah 26:18 there is a quotation from Micah 3:12. In Matthew 2:5–6 the Magi coming to Jerusalem are referred to Micah 5:2. And when Jesus sent out the Twelve he quoted Micah 7:6 (Matthew 10:35–36).

Nahum

This prophecy occurs much later than that of Micah and, instead of focusing generally upon the awful strength of the Assyrian nation, it concerns itself with the certainty of judgement upon the capital city of the Assyrians, Nineveh. Although the book is much shorter than that of Micah, it is again a mixture of justice and grace.

In response to Jonah's preaching during the eighth century BC, Nineveh had shown signs of repentance. God's threatened judgement was averted (Jonah 3:1–10) but now, in the time of Nahum, Nineveh seems to have resumed its evil ways.

The book can be divided between the themes of God's judgement and his salvation. We see God as the Judge when he warns of his righteous indignation (Nahum 1:1–6, 8–14). Chapter 2 is taken up with his threatened humiliation of the wicked city (Nahum 2:1–13) and the whole of chapter 3 deals with the justified destruction of Nineveh (Nahum 3:1–19).

The clearest glimpses of God's salvation are all perceived in chapter 1. In Nahum 1:3 the prophet speaks of the punishment of the guilty and the wonderful patience of God while he waits for sinners to repent. In Nahum 1:7 we read a precious 'gem', where God speaks of his goodness and compassion for those who are in trouble and seek his protection. Finally, in Nahum 1:12–13, 15 we learn that the affliction of God's people will come to an end and they are promised the assurance of everlasting safety.

Although Nahum is not a very well-known book, it is quoted

in the New Testament. Nahum 1:15 is cited in Acts 10:36 and Romans 10:15, and Nahum 3:4 is alluded to in Revelation 18:3.

A lesson for nations and for individuals is that 'As Nineveh sowed, so must she reap. This is God's law. Nineveh had fortified herself so that nothing could harm her. With walls 100 feet high and wide enough for four chariots to go abreast, a circumference of eighty miles, and adorned by hundreds of towers, she sat complacently. A moat 140 feet wide and sixty feet deep surrounded the vast walls. But Nineveh reckoned without Jehovah ... The mighty empire which Shalmaneser, Sargon and Sennacherib had built up, the Lord threw down with a stroke.'[3]

Those who turn their backs upon God and his Word and trust instead in physical might and political strength will find themselves in complete disarray. It is a terrible thing to disregard God and his servants. Nineveh was overthrown because of her sin (Nahum 3:1-7). She discovered that her great wealth and strength were not sufficient to save her (3:8-19).

William Hendriksen comments on this book, 'For poetic strength and beauty Nahum has no peer, unless it be Isaiah. His prophetic utterances are full of rhythm: they roll and rumble just like the chariots of war which he describes ... He predicts the downfall of *every* Nineveh that shall seek to destroy or seduce God's people. Accordingly, this prophecy forms the background of Revelation chapter seventeen.'[4]

Micah

1

The reality of judgement

Please read Micah 1:1–9

'Why are religious people frequently filled with gloom and doom?' This is a question which people often ask. They think to themselves, 'We are only on this earth for a little while. Why don't we enjoy it while we can?' Their motto is: 'Let us eat, drink and be merry, for tomorrow we die.' They do not want to be reminded of a day of judgement. They bury their heads in the sand, like ostriches. They assume that if they do not stop to think about the future, then it will go away. For them death, judgement and punishment are all taboo subjects which should be avoided because they make people feel miserable.

Micah had the same reaction to his message in his day. He had been sent by God to tell the people about the vision which 'he saw concerning Samaria and Jerusalem' (1:1). Yet when he spoke to them about the future events which were going to occur, their reaction was: 'Do not prophesy about these things; disgrace will not overtake us' (2:6).

Micah prophesied during the last half of the eighth century BC, and into the first part of the next century. He was a contemporary of Isaiah, although he may have been a little younger. Certainly he commenced his prophecy some years later than Isaiah.

Both of these prophets lived in Judah, which was the southern half of the land. The capital of Judah was Jerusalem (the home of Isaiah) while the main city of the northern kingdom was Samaria. We know that there was little love lost between these two halves of the country at that time, and the situation became worse still in later centuries. By the time of Jesus, the Jews did not even associate with the Samaritans (see John 4:9).

There are many similarities between the prophecy of Isaiah and that of Micah. However, this is not surprising since they both lived at the same time, and each of them had a great longing to see the people returning to wholehearted devotion to God. The main difference between them was that Isaiah lived in the city (indeed, he seems to have moved in court circles), while Micah was a country boy whose home was Moresheth Gath (see 1:1, 14). Micah, therefore, delivered his prophecy through the eyes of someone who lived on the hillsides which were situated about twenty-five miles southwest of the capital. Moresheth Gath probably lay something like halfway between Jerusalem and the Mediterranean coast.

Micah's prophetic utterances were delivered over a long period of time—between thirty and fifty years. His prophecy is made up of a number of oracles, or poems. His work commenced during the reign of King Jotham and he continued prophesying throughout the reign of wicked King

Ahaz. However, most of his prophecy seems to have been given during the lifetime of the godly King Hezekiah. Indeed some scholars believe that Micah may have been largely instrumental in bringing about the revival of true religion which occurred during the reign of Hezekiah.

Listen to God (1:1-2)

Micah starts with the words of the Lord. The people of the land are called upon to 'hear' and to 'listen'. This is how two other prophetic addresses begin in this book. In chapter 3:1 we read, 'Listen, you leaders of Jacob,' and in chapter 6:1 Micah says, 'Listen to [or 'hear'] what the Lord says.' This reminds us of the phrase which we read many times in the New Testament: 'He who has ears to hear, let him hear.'

Who is being called upon to listen? The prophet says, 'O peoples, all of you ... O earth and all who are in it.' So this is a message for everyone. This means that the message was not just reserved for those who lived in Israel and Judah; it sounded out to the inhabitants of the whole world. This is still the case today. The message which faithful preachers have to declare is for everyone who will take care to listen.

What makes this message so important, and why are all the peoples of the earth being called upon to take special notice of it? It is because the Sovereign Lord is speaking to everyone; and when God, the Creator and Sustainer of the whole universe, speaks then all people had better make sure that they listen.

One of the most terrible things about the people of today is that they do not want to hear what God is saying. They have no desire to pay attention to anything at all which will challenge them. They are fixed in their ways, and they are determined that nothing will change them. They will alter their habits for no one—not even God!

Micah then takes us to a scene in a law court. If we were in dire trouble and being prosecuted, and were standing in a court of law, then we would want to find people who would be able to bear witness on our behalf. We would like them to testify to our good character and our generally helpful attitude towards others. In fact, we would like to be able to find a witness who would truthfully say, 'I know he did not do it because he was with me at the time.'

Here, in verse 2, we are presented with a witness. It is the Sovereign Lord who is standing waiting to bear witness to what he knows. The solemn thing is that the witness which God is going to bring is one that is against his own people. God himself is sitting in his court of justice—that is, heaven. Micah called it, with great awe, God's 'holy temple'.

This is the setting of the first oracle that Micah delivered. He was probably preaching in the city of Jerusalem at this time. As he speaks we can well imagine the reaction of the people towards this message.

Words of judgement (1:3–4)

Micah told the people of Jerusalem what was going to happen. He said, 'Look! The Lord is coming from his dwelling-place' (1:3). When believers today hear such words they are delighted. They say, 'Christ is coming again.' Christians look forward to the glorious appearing of our Lord Jesus Christ; it is their hope. When the Lord comes back to this earth a second time it will be to deliver us from the pain and sorrow of this present evil world. But the people of Micah's day had no such hope. The prophet had not yet told them of the one who would come out of Bethlehem Ephrathah to be ruler over Israel (see 5:2).

Every one of those listening during those days in Jerusalem would have known that the phrase, 'The Lord is coming,' was an indication that the Lord was going to come with the express purpose of intervening in the affairs of men. We can read about the Lord coming down in judgement in Psalms 18:9; 96:13 and 144:5, as well as numerous times in the prophecy of Isaiah.

Micah then paints a vivid description of the effects of the Lord's coming: 'He comes down and treads the high places of the earth' (1:3). This may mean that the Lord is coming to the mountains to show that he is higher, stronger and more stable than any power. Or it may mean that he is coming down to smash to smithereens the heathen high places, those shrines where false gods and goddesses were worshipped.

The prophet further says,

'The mountains melt beneath him
and the valleys split apart,
like wax before the fire,
like water rushing down a slope'   (1:4).

Leslie Allen comments, 'Micah uses this terrifying poetry to build up an impression of God's irresistible power directed in catastrophe against his enemies.'[1]

The purpose of God's coming (1:5–7)

Micah told the people that 'All this is because of Jacob's transgression, because of the sins of the house of Israel.' We can almost hear the people in Micah's audience beginning to tut-tut and shake their heads in a knowing way. We can imagine them saying, 'I feared that our northern neighbours [Israel] would go too far. They have sinned against the laws of God once too often and now, quite rightly, the Lord is going to punish them.'

They would think this because of what was actually happening around them. Everyone knew that the Assyrian army was threatening Samaria; and it could only be a matter of time before the northern kingdom fell under its onslaughts. Amos had warned them: 'Woe to you who are complacent ... who feel secure on Mount Samaria' (Amos 6:1). Now that things were hotting up for Israel, God was going to punish them severely and he was going to use the dreaded Assyrians to demonstrate his displeasure. 'You can't say that they haven't been warned,' is what Micah's hearers might well have said.

What is Jacob's transgression which is spoken of here? Micah gives us the answer: 'Is it not Samaria?' (1:5). Samaria was guilty because she had been unfaithful to God. She had indulged herself in pleasure rather than in wholehearted obedience to God's commands. Verse 7 says, 'since she gathered her gifts from the wages of prostitutes, as the wages of prostitutes they will again be used.'

Prostitution is often used in the Scriptures as a picture of infidelity to God. When a nation, or an individual, went after false gods it is often likened to a husband turning his back upon his wife and seeking pleasure in a woman of the street. Ezekiel spoke about a similar case: 'For this is what the Sovereign Lord says: I am about to hand you over to those you hate, to those you turned away from in disgust. They will deal with you in hatred and take away everything you have worked for. They will leave you naked and bare, and the shame of your prostitution will be exposed. Your lewdness and promiscuity have brought this upon you, because you lusted after the nations and defiled yourself with their idols' (Ezekiel 23:28–30).

Micah then told his hearers what God was going to do to the disobedient people. He said, 'I will make Samaria a heap of rubble' (1:6). When I read these words it brings to my mind a picture of what London looked like in the blitz (the massive bombing of the early days of the Second World War). London was a mess of broken and ruined houses; indeed, some parts of it remained so for some years after the end of the war.

God said that Samaria, which had been a great city with grand buildings in it, would become like a bomb-site. After the judgement of God the city would be flattened. It would only be fit to be 'a place for planting vineyards' (1:6).

Micah goes on to give a more detailed description of what the Lord was going to do to Samaria. He says, 'I will pour her stones into the valley.' The once proud city which had been built upon a hill (1 Kings 16:24) would be thrown down into a valley. In fact her stones would be poured into the valley just 'like water rushing down a slope' (cf. 1:4). All that would be left after the destruction would be the foundations of the once grand city but even they would be poking through the violently disturbed earth. God said,

'All her idols will be broken to pieces;
all her temple gifts will be burned with fire;
I will destroy all her images'   (1:7).

This verse takes us to the root of all of Samaria's sin. Her idolatry, which took her away from the worship of the true God, will not only be worthless; it will be utterly destroyed by fire (as nature itself will melt 'like wax before the fire' of God's judgement—see 1:4). At that time the money which had been earned by prostitutes would be taken and reused. The prophet seems to mean that 'The wealth that Samaria had gained from her idolatry will be taken by the Assyrians and placed in their own temples, to be used again in the worship of idols.'[2]

Judah's fate (1:8–9)
To those in Jerusalem, who were feeling very smug that Samaria was going to be punished so severely, Micah says words to this effect: 'You can see the sin of Samaria and you know that

Jacob's transgression is the sin of Samaria (1:5). but what about yourselves?' Was Judah completely faultless? No, it was far from perfect. And then, with penetrating accuracy, the voice of Micah cried out, 'What is Judah's high place? Is it not Jerusalem?' (1:5). He means that the holy city of Jersualem, to which the people of the southern kingdom looked in awe and reverence, was nothing other than a pagan centre of idolatry. It is true that Samaria was going to be destroyed and her citizens taken away as captives, never to return; but Jerusalem, too, will not escape the judgement. 'Her wound is incurable.' The disease of Samaria's sin will also come to Judah. This is the burden of Micah's message: 'The Lord wants to alert you to the danger you are in.' This is why he says, 'It [the judgement] has reached the very gate of my people, even to Jerusalem itself' (1:9).

History tells us that the Assyrian army did come right up to the walls of Jerusalem, as Micah graphically put it, to 'the very gate'. Gates of ancient cities were very important. It was there that justice was meted out! It was all very well for Jerusalem to condemn Samaria for its sin, but how holy were the people of the southern kingdom? The answer was that they were as bad as those who lived in the north, and they too would be judged by the Lord.

The apostle Peter tells us, 'It is time for judgement to begin with the family of God.' He also adds, 'And if it begins with us, what will the outcome be for those who do not obey the gospel of God?' (1 Peter 4:17).

Our response

What did Micah do? He performed a visual parable. He tells them,

'Because of this [coming judgement] I will weep and wail.
I will go about barefoot and naked.

I will howl like a jackal
and moan like an owl'   (1:8).

Micah acted dramatically, as Ezekiel sometimes did, to draw the people's attention to the dire straits that they were in (see Ezekiel chapters 4 and 5).

Micah dressed himself only in a loincloth (which was as bad as being totally naked), and he walked stripped and barefoot through Jerusalem. He also howled like a jackal and moaned like an owl. The prophet of God did all this to demonstrate the awfulness of the sin of Samaria—indeed, the sin of all of God's people.

These things may seem almost laughable to us, but we are foolish if we do snigger at them. Britain, in common with many other nations, is guilty of very grave sins. We are not only guilty of turning our backs upon God and his commands, but we are condemned because we put our own desires before the will of God. Most of all, we are guilty of the heinous sin of failing to heed the warnings which God continually gives us that he will not overlook our sin.

The Lord's name will be vindicated, and he will regain his rightful place among the people. Paul tells us that one day,

'At the name of Jesus every knee [shall] bow,
in heaven and on earth and under the earth,
and every tongue confess that Jesus Christ is Lord'
                                    (Philippians 2:10–11).

It may be that there is someone who is reading this book who has never been convicted of his or her sin. If so, then the solemn fact is that '[Your] wound is incurable' (1:9). There is no hope for you in the state that you are in. Judgement is even now lurking at your door. The only escape for you is to become a new man or woman by turning to the Lord Jesus Christ in repentance of your sin, and trusting him for your salvation. Those who want to escape the judgement of God 'must be born again' (John 3:3, 7).

However, Christians are not let off God's punishment completely. God says, '[Judgement] has reached the very gate of my people' (1:9). He says, 'My people need to repent and turn again to me.' He is a foolish person who 'invokes a blessing on himself and therefore thinks, "I will be safe, even though I persist in going my own way"' (Deuteronomy 29:19).

2

Sin and its consequences

Please read Micah 1:10–16

These verses record Micah's second oracle to the people of Jerusalem. This oracle (or poem) seems to have been delivered quite a number of years after the one recorded in verses 2–9. By this time it would seem that Samaria had already fallen to the Assyrians and a great many of its inhabitants had been deported. From the Assyrians' own records we can learn that they treated their captives very badly. Presumably the people of Samaria were also abused; certainly they never returned to their land. This is why the people of the northern kingdom are sometimes called 'the ten lost tribes'.

In this section we see Micah pondering upon the trouble which he saw lying ahead for the towns and villages where he had been brought up. These places had, for centuries, plodded on in their country ways. However, as the prophet considered each of the names of these places he realized that they held a new and sinister significance. In the series of puns which he made upon the names of the villages and towns his hearers would have understood that these warnings should be taken with deadly seriousness.

Micah is ashamed (1:10)

Micah's home village was Moresheth Gath; it was situated some twenty-five miles south-west of Jerusalem. There, in the foothills of Judah, were a sprinkling of settlements, and Micah would have been very familiar with each of these towns because they were in the region where he grew up. The whole of that area overlooked the coastal plain where the Philistines lived.

Because they were high up, the people of these villages would have been able to look down and observe the comings and goings along the main road which led from the north down to Egypt, a great distance to the south. They would also have known of the various alliances which the kings of Judah had made with the Egyptians. They may well have been aware, too, of what God thought about these friendships. Perhaps they had heard what Isaiah had prophesied: 'Those who trusted in Cush [Upper Egypt], and boasted in Egypt [lower Egypt—i.e. the area around the Giza Pyramids and the Nile delta] will be afraid and put to shame. In that day the people who live on this coast will say, "See what has happened to those we relied on, those we fled to for help and deliverance from the king of Assyria! How then can we escape?"' (Isaiah 20:5–6).

These villagers may also have heard Isaiah's warning:

'Woe to those who go down to Egypt for help,
who rely on horses,
who trust in the multitude of their chariots
and in the great strength of their horsemen,
but do not look to the Holy One of Israel,
or seek help from the Lord'   (Isaiah 31:1).

It was because of the unholy alliances that the leaders of Judah had made that Micah said, 'Tell it not in Gath; weep not at all' (1:10). He meant, 'Don't draw attention to the terrible state of our beloved land.' He said this because he did not want to make the enemies of Judah aware of the dreadful condition of the country. He was ashamed of the state of his country, but he had no desire to give more ammunition to those who wished to harm God's people. He did not wish to give them information so that they could attack the land even earlier than they had planned to do.

However, does this mean that Micah thought that the sin of the people could be ignored or shut away? Certainly not. By the language he used, we can see how upset he was. He said, 'Tell it not in Gath.' The Hebrew word for 'Gath' sounds like the word for 'tell'. So Micah was making a play on words here. He was saying, in effect, 'Tell it not in "Telltown".' He seems to mean, 'Despite the name of this place, keep quiet about what is going on. To think about the Assyrians invading our land is too awful to contemplate. It is so unspeakable that it ought to stun us into silence.'

But there is also another echo here. The phrase, 'Tell it not in Gath,' would have reminded the people of a poem which harked back to the glorious former King of Israel, great King David. The people must have often thought about that wonderful age when David ruled in the land, and just to hear his name mentioned would have brought great encouragement to them. Also, when Micah mentioned the name 'Adullam' in verse 15, it would have caused them to remember their former king and no doubt to do so with great affection.

Their joy would have been short-lived, however, because both of these allusions to David refer to extremely sad times in his life. When David sang, 'Tell it not in Gath,' he was lamenting the death of King Saul and the heir to the throne, Jonathan (see 2 Samuel 1:20). Jonathan was a particularly good friend of David, and 'Tell it not in Gath,' was part of David's lament for the king and his son.

The mention of Adullam would have made the people recall the earlier time when David had been living in the Cave of Adullam as a fugitive, hunted by King Saul (1 Samuel 22:1–2). This first king of Israel had become very jealous of David and he had tried many times to kill him. So, for some time David had to hide as a common fugitive in a cave—and the name of the cave was Adullam. While David lived there a great number of other outlawed people flocked to his side. So these allusions to King David were far from joyful ones.

Twelve towns of Judah (1:10–15)

At the mention of each of these towns, a different aspect of the judgement of God is highlighted for the attention of Micah's hearers. After Gath, Micah speaks of Beth Ophrah. He tells this town to 'roll in the dust' (1:10). This was one of the signs of a repentant spirit. We often read of people in the Old Testament clothing themselves in sackcloth and ashes. Micah is talking about the same idea here. Dust was placed on the head as a sign of sorrow (Job 2:12; Revelation 18:19) and of contrition (Joshua 7:6). Something similar is referred to in the New Testament. There Jesus spoke about giving a warning of judgement by shaking the dust off the feet when the disciples left a town where their message had not been received.[1] Here it is the inhabitants of Beth Ophrah (which sounds like the Hebrew word for 'dust') who are told to roll in the dust because of the awful calamity which is going to come upon them.

Next the prophet addressed some remarks to the inhabitants of Shaphir. The Hebrew word for this name sounds like another word which means 'beautiful'. So Micah said that these people who lived in '"Fairtown" will march away as prisoners of war, ignominiously stripped of their fine clothes'.[2] In fact, when they leave the land, they will be far from beautiful.

Then Micah names two towns where cowards live. He said of Zaanan that they 'will not come out' (1:11). However, the name 'Zaanan' suggests the similar-sounding word which does mean 'go out'. Yet, when the Assyrian army comes, Micah said these very people will betray the name of their own town. They will be afraid to come out and fight. They will remain shut up, in hiding. Beth Ezel will not fight the invaders either. The inhabitants of the town will be too busy mourning to make any attempt to protect the countryside round about it (1:11).

We see then, that the judgement which will come upon the land will be so great that the whole population will long for deliverance. This is why Micah says, 'Those who live in Maroth writhe in pain, waiting for relief' (1:12). The meaning of the word Maroth is 'to grieve' or 'to expect'. The prophet seems to be saying here, 'When the Assyrians come they will bring disaster, and this will be at the instigation of the Lord. In fact, there will be nothing to alleviate the grieving of the people; they will wait expectantly, but it will all be in vain.' Calvin says that the judgement will come 'that the Jews [in the south] as well as the Israelites [in the north], might know that they had to do, not with men only, but also with God, the celestial Judge'.[3]

After all of this tale of woe, Micah turns to the citizens of the capital and tells them that disaster will come 'even to the gate of Jerusalem' (1:12). Jerusalem is the city of peace; that is what the word means. But, because of the backsliding of its people (1:5), this city, which signifies 'blessing', will have disaster creep up to its very walls. 'It is striking that Sennacherib, who overran Judah, some years later, speaks in his annals of Hezekiah "shut up like a caged bird" in his beleaguered city so that "any who went out of its city gate" was turned back.'[4]

So why, in this chapter which is filled with the smell of the coming judgement of God upon sin, do we twice have mention of the gate of Jerusalem? (1:9, 12). The gate of any city was where the law was carried out; it was the place of justice. Does not the gate of Jerusalem remind us of the place where the Lord Jesus Christ went out of the city on his way to be crucified some 700 years after Micah prophesied? Jesus was crucified outside the city wall. It was there that God's justice (in judgement against sin) and God's mercy (in forgiveness of the penitent) was carried out. This thought is summed up so well in the lovely hymn:

Beneath the cross of Jesus
I fain would take my stand ...

The second verse goes:

O safe and happy shelter!
O refuge tried and sweet!
O trysting-place where heaven's love
And heaven's justice meet.[5]

So the disaster, which was to come upon the nation, was intended to bring the people to true repentance for their sin (see 1:8–9, 16).

In verse 13 the important city of Lachish is mentioned. Archaeologists have dug up many instructive 'finds' in this city, and none of them contradicts what is recorded in the Scriptures. Lachish lay some thirty miles south-west of Jerusalem. That was another five or six miles further on from Micah's home town of Moresheth Gath. It was part of the defence system built to protect Judah from Egyptian or Philistine attack (2 Chronicles 11:5–12). Much of their security relied on powerful war horses and chariots of Lachish. The name Lachish means 'team' in Hebrew, so it has been called 'Horse-town' by F.W. Farrar.[6] Micah calls upon Lachish to 'harness the team [of horses] to the chariot' (1:13).

Horses would have been kept for the purposes of war. But Micah is calling upon the inhabitants to harness their horses to the chariots, not to fight, but to flee from, their enemy. They were going to want to gallop away because of their sin. The prophet said, 'The transgressions of Israel [meaning the whole land—north and south] were found in you' (1:13).

What was their sin? It was to put their faith in the efficacy of their horses and chariots, rather than in the power of God. Because Lachish was guilty of trusting in human defences rather than in the Lord, she would lose one of her towns, Moresheth Gath. As he spoke these words, Micah must have been particularly saddened because Moresheth Gath was his own home town. In Hebrew the name of this town sounds very much like the word for 'betrothed'. Therefore, when Micah said, 'You will give parting gifts to Moresheth Gath' (1:14) he was probably thinking of a girl leaving her family and coming under the new authority of her husband.[7] Only, in the case of Moresheth Gath, the town would have to pay tribute to the invader (a kind of dowry). Also it would see many of its townspeople taken away into exile.

Likewise 'The town of Aczib will prove deceptive to the kings of Israel' (1:14). In this case the town would be true to its name, 'deception' (cf. Jeremiah 15:18). Aczib would become a false possession of the kings of Israel because it would come to be owned by a foreign king.

At this point Micah looks towards the south again and he pictures Mareshah in his mind's eye (1:15). This was another important frontier town, also part of Rehoboam's defence system (2 Chronicles 11:6-10). It would be a rich prize for any invader, because it would open up the way into the interior of Judah. However, Micah says that Mareshah (which means 'possessor' or 'heir') will be taken over by a new heir. It will be conquered by the enemy.

Lastly, we read, 'He who is the glory of Israel will come to Adullam' (1:15). Just as in the days of King David many people fled to his care, so in the days of judgement, which would soon come, the aristocracy of the land (the glory of Israel) would seek to find safety behind the ramparts of Adullam.

In a similar way we read about the great Judgement Day which is still in the future, yet which will come upon this earth. At that time, 'The kings of the earth, the princes, the generals, the rich, the mighty, and every slave and every free man [will hide] in caves and among the rocks of the mountains. They [will call] to the mountains and the rocks, "Fall on us and hide us from the wrath of the Lamb! For the great day of their wrath has come, and who can stand?"' (Revelation 6:15-17).

What can be done? (1:16)

Micah says, 'Shave your heads in mourning for the children in whom you delight' (1:16). As at the end of the first oracle, Micah calls upon the people to mourn because of their sin (cf. 1:8-9). The prophet had been upset enough when he spoke of the wound of Jerusalem (her sin) being incurable. He says, 'It has reached the very gate of my people' (1:9). And if he called the citizens of Jerusalem 'my people', what must have been his reaction to the judgement which was about to come on the area of the country where he had grown up? This judgement would grievously affect his own friends, acquaintances and relations.

When the Israelites mourned it was their custom to shave

their hair (it was normally worn long by both sexes); but on this occasion, because the sin of the people was so great, Micah urged them to shave the whole of their heads. They were to make themselves look like the griffin-vulture, whose white down-covered head made it look completely bald. This was a sign of great shame and sorrow.

I remember what happened to the young women of Paris who, during the war, had gone out with the men of the German occupying forces. When the city was liberated these young women were rounded up by the Parisians who shaved off all their beautiful long hair. They were then forced to parade through me streets of the city bald, in shame; while everyone jeered at them.

Micah next highlighted what was going to happen to the children. He says, 'They will go from you into exile' (1:16). Can any of us think of a more dreadful thing for a parent to bear than to see his own children forcibly taken from him and deported to a foreign country?

The meaning for us
We may find this passage difficult to understand, but it is the Word of God so it must be taken seriously. Micah is not playing clever word-games just for the amusement of his listeners. He is in deadly earnest. He is speaking about the danger which was even then awaiting them from the Assyrian army—an army which would shortly be at their doors. The prophet is saying, 'The Lord God Almighty is going to bring great judgement upon you because of your sin.'

Stuart Briscoe, writing for an American readership, puts these things in his contemporary situation by saying, 'Imagine an American preacher saying, "Living in Pittsburgh is the pits", or "Los Angeles is no city of angels" or "Wisconsin should only be pronounced Wiscon-*sin*!"' Briscoe says, 'That would get the people's attention.'[8]

It is the responsibility of every believer to urge people to listen to the warnings of God's Word. Like Ezekiel, we are all, to some extent, 'watchmen' whose responsibility it is to warn the unsaved person of the danger he or she is in. If we fail to use every means within our power (including, maybe, puns) to arrest the attention of the unconverted, then the Lord says to us, 'That wicked man will die for his sin, and I will hold you accountable for his blood' (Ezekiel 3:18).

The point is that God is angry about sin, and just as Israel and Judah were punished because of their unfaithfulness to God, so shall we be. That knowledge should make us tremble. It should make us cry out, 'How then can we escape?' (Isaiah 20:6). Is there a refuge to which we can flee to find safety from the judgement which is coming upon us because of our sin? Yes, there is a place in which to hide—that is the good news of the gospel. There is hope. The only place of deliverance is in the Lord Jesus Christ, God's Son. He went all the way to the cross of Calvary to take upon himself the judgement of God for sin. As Anne Cousin writes,

> O Christ what burdens bowed thy head!
> Our load was laid on thee;
> Thou stoodest in the sinner's stead,
> Didst bear all ill for me.
> A victim led, thy blood was shed!
> Now there's no load for me.

> Death and the curse were in our cup:
> O Christ 'twas full for thee!
> But thou hast drained the last dark drop,
> 'Tis empty now for me.

That bitter cup, love drank it up,
Now blessing's draught for me.

Jehovah lifted up his rod:
O Christ, it fell on thee!
Thou wast sore stricken of thy God;
There's not one stroke for me.
Thy tears, thy blood, beneath it flowed;
Thy bruising healeth me.[9]

3

Our plans—and God's!

Please read Micah 2:1-13

Ever since the end of the Second World War certain parts of Great Britain (especially in more populous areas) had been designated as Green Belt land. This was done to stop any building work taking place in these parts which might have ruined the natural countryside. However, during the 1980s much of south-east England (and perhaps other parts of Britain as well) started to sprout with buildings—many of them ugly and untidy. The work which went on was so prolific that the open country between each town started to shrink in size, despite the fact that much of this land had been designated as Green Belt. This situation had largely come about because developers had seized the opportunity to buy up land fairly cheaply, erect houses, hotels and office blocks, and then sell them off at enormous profit to themselves.

This kind of thing is not new, though. Isaiah had something

to say about activities of this kind. He spoke to the 'opportunists' of about 2,700 years ago and said,

> 'Woe to you who add house to house
> and join field to field
> till no space is left'   (Isaiah 5:8).

Micah, likewise, elaborated on the reasons why so much of the land area was used up. In his day this came about as a result of the plans of greedy people who were already wealthy and who wanted to get wealthier still.

Greedy rich people (2:1–5)

Rich men planned how they could become richer still, but Paul tells us that 'The love of money is a root of all kinds of evil' (1 Timothy 6:10). If our main aim in life is to make as much money as we possibly can then we too are foolish. Most really rich people tend to be very miserable. John D. Rockerfeller said, 'The poorest man I know is the man who has nothing but money.'[1]

In Micah's day rich men did not sleep very well (2:1). We know this to be true because the prophet tells us that instead of using their beds for rest and refreshment (as they were meant to do) they stayed awake all night planning how to increase their wealth. They were, therefore, abusing God's gift of sleep; and anyone who misuses any of God's precious gifts is heading for trouble.

These rich men plotted evil on their beds, but that was not the whole story. Their idea was to increase their wealth by illegitimate means. Micah tells us that they planned iniquity. He meant that they broke the tenth commandment, which says, 'You shall not covet your neighbour's house. You shall not covet your neighbour's wife, or his manservant or maidservant, or his ox or his donkey, or anything that belongs to your neighbour' (Exodus 20:17).

When anyone plans iniquity, plots evil and longs to have something which does not belong to him, then he is going to do everything in his power to obtain what he has set his heart upon. The sin of coveting is very subtle. The more we long to have something which belongs to someone else, the more we are going to be obsessed by the importance of possessing it. We can illustrate this by thinking about how a man or woman who starts to covet the looks, the charm or the excitement of someone else's wife or husband is likely to behave. If such people persist in their coveting then they are heading for the divorce courts. Everyone should beware of the sin of coveting anything which rightly belongs to another person.

However, God's laws did not seem to mean very much to the rich people whom Micah denounced. These men disobeyed God's laws. In fact, they could hardly wait to put their greedy schemes into operation. As soon as it was light they arose from their beds and set to work. Micah tells us, 'At morning's light they carry ... out [their plan] because it is in their power to do it' (2:1). They seize the fields they have lain awake all night thinking about. 'They defraud a man of his home, a fellow-man of his inheritance' (2:2). These actions are very intense. Think of the violence associated with Micah's words, 'seize', 'take' and 'defraud'.

How could these rich men get away with such injustice? Presumably it was because they were powerful, greedy, influential and determined. To understand the importance attached to the concept of Israel's family inheritance let us think about the story of Naboth's vineyard. King Ahab wanted Naboth's vineyard because it was close to the palace. The king did not want the land for nothing. He was prepared to give a fair price for it, but Naboth, who was presumably a loyal subject, said, 'The Lord forbid that I should give you the inheritance of my fathers' (1 Kings 21:3).

Naboth was not being rude to the king; he was merely adhering to the God-given laws of inheritance. In ancient Israel all of the land belonged, not to the people, but to the Lord. However, every family was allocated a portion of it to work and care for as stewards of God's earth. This is the reason why Naboth could not give up his vineyard, however attractive the price might have been, even though his refusal ultimately cost him his life. The awful thing was that the greedy men of Micah's time completely overlooked God's laws. Regardless of what God had said about the matter, they plotted to have the land for themselves; and they took it without any regard for the fear of God or the justice of the people's case.[2] Because they were powerful, rich and influential in the country, they trod down the poor, and no one dared to speak against them.

However, that was not the end of the story. These rich men were not the only ones who had been planning. God had his plans too, and no one can overthrow or ignore the Lord's programme. He is the supreme Ruler over all things. Those who ignore this fact do so at their peril. God said, 'I am planning disaster against this people' (2:3). In calling them 'this people', not 'my people' (see also 2:11), he showed he was disowning them on account of their disobedience to his commandments, and because they had broken the covenant that he had made with them (see Deuteronomy 26:17–18). It was these wealthy men who, by their own actions, had cut themselves off from the Lord.

Then Micah told the rich people more about the trouble which was going to come upon them. He said that they would not be able to save themselves from the calamity which would befall them. Up till then their money, their power and influence had obtained for them everything that they desired. But, from that point onwards, everything was going to be different.

They would be toppled from their exalted positions. They would no longer walk around in a proud manner (2:3). Rather, for them, it would be a time of calamity. They would be ridiculed by others and tormented with a mournful song:

'We are utterly ruined;
My people's possession is divided up.
He takes it from me!
He assigns our fields to the traitors'   (2:4).

This disaster, calamity and ruin would be brought about by the invaders who would would assign the land to those whom the Judeans would think of as belonging to the lower classes. They would consider these common people to be unholy and, therefore, traitors. We can imagine the rest of the Judeans, particularly the landowners, were very upset because they would be the ones who would lose their land for ever. Isaiah also comments on this situation in Isaiah 33:1.

Every fifty years in Israel was a year of jubilee. In this year all land was returned to those families to whom it had originally been entrusted. When the reallocation took place each family who had a claim on any part of the land would be able to send a representative to the assembly. However, the Lord said that these particular rich, greedy men would have no one to represent them in the assembly of the Lord (2:5). Presumably the Lord would ban them from this important ceremony.

Therefore justice would be done. God would be vindicated. We find the same thing expressed in the New Testament, where Paul warns us, 'Do not be deceived: God cannot be mocked. A man reaps what he sows' (Galatians 6:7). The message for us all is that we must make sure that we do not put our own desires before our obedience to the law of the Lord.

Prophets who were false (2:6–11)

Whenever anyone speaks up for God, there will be many more who will denounce what is said as old-fashioned, irrelevant and untrue. But the rich people did not want to ignore God altogether. No doubt they rationalized their actions by saying, 'What we are doing will benefit the people.'

I suppose we have the same thing today when, as happened to many communities in my part of Britain in the 1980s, large supermarket chains donated many thousands of pounds to build a community centre or a better road—just so that they could win the approval of the local council planning department and gain permission to build a large store in a prime location. In some countries this kind of thing would be called bribery.

The rich men of Micah's day had their own prophets, whom they presumably paid well for their work. These prophets complained about Micah. They said that it was he who was the false prophet. They said to him, 'Do not prophesy about these things; disgrace will not overtake us.' They went on to say, 'God is not as you say he is. Is the Spirit of the Lord angry? Does he do such things?' (2:7).

These false prophets were saying, as many people do today, 'God is a God of love. We are all going to go to heaven anyway, so it doesn't matter too much how we behave. Don't talk to us about hell and judgement. That's not my idea of what God is like.' Yet how deluded these people are! God is not someone whom God's people have dreamed up in their own imaginations. He is real, he is powerful and he is angry against all sin, and all sinners.

Then Micah went on to give further details about the

methods these rich people used to reclaim their debts. He said they did it with violence. Those who owed them money were pounced upon, perhaps by gangs of debt collectors hired by the wealthy.[3] These mobs forcibly removed their outer robes as though they were fighting in a battle with an enemy. But Micah said that they were breaking God's commandments. The prophet was not saying that people should not repay their debts, but he was urging that these things should be done in a reasonable and fair way. These men, who were already rich, were ignoring God's commands of Exodus 22:26-27: 'If you take your neighbour's cloak as a pledge, return it to him by sunset, because his cloak is the only covering he has for his body. What else will he sleep in?' (See also Deuteronomy 24:10-13).

Micah pointed out that violence was also done to the women (probably widows) and their children as well. He said,

'You drive the women of my people
from their pleasant homes.
You take away my blessing
from their children for ever'   (2:9).

It seems that these women rightfully owned their homes, but the rich men had somehow come to acquire them and, in a way totally contrary to God's laws, forcibly evicted the women. Widows and orphans always have a special place in the care of God. Yet these wealthy landowners ignored the compassion which God shows to such people. Jesus himself criticized those who 'devour widows' houses and for a show make lengthy prayers' (Mark 12:40).

There is a parallel today. Many people, as I write this, have been turned out of their homes because they have not been able to keep up their mortgage payments. Often this has come about because greedy people have forced up the prices of houses and played the money-market. As a result, things like high interest rates and unexpected unemployment have caused many householders to end up in a sad, homeless condition. Likewise there have been many who have taught that God rewards (financially and with good health) those who give everything to him (or, rather, to the preacher). These 'preachers' are sometimes referred to as 'health, wealth and prosperity' preachers. A Greek friend of mine told me that one of these men travelled through his area some years ago and persuaded a poor farmer to sell up everything and, in return, he promised that God would grant the man great blessings. Today that farmer is a bankrupt and disillusioned man!

What does God say to those behind these injustices? 'Get up, go away! For this is not your resting place, because it is defiled' (2:10). These people thought that they lived in the promised land, the land of rest, but God said, 'This is not your resting place. You don't deserve the benefits of my land, or any of the other blessings which I have for my people. Get out and go away!'

They were also guilty of only wanting to hear good things spoken by the prophets. They only wanted to know about those things which would satisfy their baser desires. Micah said, 'If a liar and deceiver comes and says, "I will prophesy for you plenty of wine and beer," he would be just the prophet for this people!' (2:11). 'What more could one expect of this people?' Micah contemptuously implies. 'You are no longer God's people if you behave like this.'

The scene brightens (2:12–13)
There is a saying in English which goes, 'Not everyone is tarred with the same brush.' This means that in a large group of people not everyone will be guilty of the same faults. It was not all bad news. When Micah spoke to the faithful remnant of God's

people he gave them good news. Not everyone was greedy, selfish and disobedient to God's laws. Not everyone had turned their backs upon the principles of justice and righteousness. Not everyone had wandered away from the Shepherd of Israel. There were some who had remained true to the flock of God.

Despite all the calamities which were going to come upon the land because of the invading Assyrians, there would be a deliverance. God had heard their cry, the bleating of his sheep.[4] The Lord said, through his servant,

'I will surely gather all of you, O Jacob;
I will surely bring together the remnant of Israel.
I will bring them together like sheep in a pen,
like a flock in its pasture;
the place will throng with people'   (2:12).

This is a very positive message. Over and over again God says, 'I will ...', and when God says, 'I will,' he does! The Lord spoke of those who are faithful to him being guarded by the Shepherd of the sheep (John 10:2-4). These come from Jacob and from the remnant of Israel. He means people from both parts of the land. God is seen in Psalm 78:52-53 as the one who 'brought his people out like a flock; he led his sheep through the desert. He guided them safely, so they were unafraid.' Obviously this psalm initially referred to the deliverance of the children of Israel from Egypt, but it also looked forward to prophecies such as this one. This prophecy is seen clearly fulfilled in the Lord Jesus Christ who, as the Good Shepherd, speaks of bringing his people into the security of the pen (the sheepfold of God).

The Lord spoke of this in John 10:14-18 where he said, 'I am the good shepherd; I know my sheep and my sheep know me— just as the Father knows me and I know the Father—and I lay down my life for the sheep. I have other sheep that are not of this sheep pen. I must bring them also. They too will listen to my voice, and there shall be one flock and one shepherd. The reason my Father loves me is that I lay down my life—only to take it up again. No one takes it from me, but I lay it down of my own accord. I have authority to lay it down and authority to take it up again. This command I received from my Father.'

The picture now changes to describe the Mighty One who was going to win the victory for God's people. Micah said,

'One who breaks open the way will go up before them;
they will break through the gate and go out.
Their king will pass through before them,
the Lord at their head'   (2:13).

In these verses we see now, not a gentle Shepherd, but a strong and powerful King who will break down all barriers and open up the way for his people to enter into all the blessings of God. This is the Messiah in his role as the conqueror of sin and also as the King of kings and Lord of lords.

For some while, the Assyrian army had been surrounding Jerusalem. Their king had long held sway over them. One day Sennacherib, the Assyrian king, taunted Hezekiah, King of Judah, and said, 'Do not let the god you depend on deceive you when he says, "Jerusalem will not be handed over to the king of Assyria' " (2 Kings 19:10). However, this heathen ruler was wrong. After Hezekiah had read a letter from him, and spread it before the Lord in the temple, 'The angel of the Lord went out and put to death a hundred and eighty-five thousand men in the Assyrian camp ... So Sennacherib king of Assyria broke camp and withdrew. He returned to Nineveh [his capital city] and stayed there.' A little later this great king was murdered by two of his sons and one of them ruled in his place (2 Kings 19:35-37).

Although Jerusalem had been delivered—for the time

being—that did not mean that God had changed his mind about bringing judgement upon the people of God. He merely withheld his hand for a while. He had said that calamity would come upon the evil people of the land, and all those who refused to repent of their sin would certainly be punished severely. However, God graciously gave them longer to come to their senses. Jerusalem would be destroyed, but not yet!

The certainty of judgement upon sin
God has declared that judgement will come upon all who disobey him, but he has graciously held back from carrying out his punishment. Why is that? It is because he is 'not wanting anyone to perish, but everyone to come to repentance' (2 Peter 3:9).

This is a message for everyone today. We may not be rich, but does the acquisition of money, power and possessions captivate our minds? Do we honestly have a desire to keep God's laws, even if we miss out financially? Are we concerned only to listen to God's voice, or do we want to pay attention to religious people who tell us things that we want to hear? Do we love the Lord with all our heart, strength and soul, or do we love ourselves most of all?

4

Justice and righteousness

Please read Micah 3:1–12

What kind of people are given the most startling headlines in our newspapers, and other media? It is the thief, the terrorist and the adulterer. These are the sorts of people who have their stories displayed in very prominent positions. Their wicked deeds are advertised widely and there seems to be no shortage of people eager to read about them.

However, stories about those who perform acts of kindness, love and gentleness are usually relegated to the inside pages of our newspapers (if they are mentioned at all); and even then they often appear on pages 4, 6 or 8, where they will not immediately be seen as the reader opens his paper.

We have a strange system for praising heroes and heroines. It was not one which was followed by the prophets of the Old Testament. Isaiah, a contemporary of Micah, denounced those whose moral values were upside down. He said,

'Woe to those who call evil good
and good evil,
who put darkness for light
and light for darkness,
who put bitter for sweet
and sweet for bitter'   (Isaiah 5:20).

Micah also speaks about the same kind of people in chapter
3:2 of his prophecy. However, the ones for whom both Isaiah and
Micah reserved their strongest condemnation were the leaders
of the nation. The prophets came down most heavily upon these
men because they had been placed in positions of authority; it
was their responsibility to lead those who were under them into
right ways. Instead of doing that, they were abusing the trust
which had been solemnly placed upon them.

The sins of the leaders (3:1-4)

Micah commences this opening section of chapter 3 with a
statement. In very emphatic tones he utters, 'Then I said' (3:1).
Following this we read what must be a summary of Micah's
work. As he prophesied in Judah for something like forty years,
it follows that this short book called 'Micah' can only contain
a small selection of his work. We have already seen that he
preached during the reigns of three of Judah's kings. If we
examine what happened throughout that time we discover
that the people sinned over and over again. Like Israel all
throughout its history, these Judeans committed the same kind
of transgressions of God's law time without number. This is the
reason why the prophets continuously denounced the evil of the
people.

Therefore we, for our part, must not grow weary of hearing
sinful ways being condemned; we should never tire of listening
to the voice of God. Just as the prophets of those days spent
much of their time denouncing the things that were being done

against the Lord and his law, so preachers of today must also concentrate on condemning the evil which is being committed in our days. It is all too easy for those who declare God's Word to speak out against sins which are, in general, not being committed by the congregation which sits in front of them week after week. How many sermons are preached in which things like Sunday trading, drunkenness and gambling are condemned while, by and large, Christian people are not indulging in these things? For a preacher to concentrate only upon things in which those outside of the church are engaged merely leaves his hearers feeling smug and self-righteous because they are not guilty of these activities.

Preachers today should be like the prophets of old and denounce God's people because of the sins which they are committing. Here are some of the things Christian people have always been guilty of: pride, selfishness and a love of the 'limelight'. Congregations should be shamed into admitting their uncharitableness towards others and their intolerance of those who have not been brought up in the ways of Christ. How awful it is when believers frown at a newcomer because he or she is not dressed as they would wish, or does not know his way around the Bible!

Preachers today must not take the easy way out, as the false prophets did in Micah's day (see 3:5). They should not give the impression that there is nothing wrong with the professing people of God today. They should be active in pointing out that the lives of Christians are not as they should be; there is a great deal wrong in the church of our days.

The issues which are outlined in these verses are matters which Micah addressed many, many times. But it was the leaders of the land whom he reprimanded in the first instance. It was they who had responsibility for the spiritual, moral and physical welfare of the people and they should always carry out their duties diligently. Micah told the leaders to 'listen' because he was going to say something to them which was very important. When he spoke it was imperative that they took notice of the message because it came straight from God himself.

When a nation's leaders ignore what God says, then all of the people are likely to suffer. The same can be said of the church. Those of us who hold positions of leadership in God's church must take care that we carry out all of our duties carefully. There is a great responsibility laid upon everyone who serves in the church. There are some who have ignored the teaching of Peter in 1 Peter 5:3 and who do '[lord] it over those entrusted to [them]'. Those who engage in so-called 'heavy shepherding' have sometimes ordered that the members of the churches they lead should follow them blindly, without questioning any of the instructions which they may give. Such pastors will have much to answer for on the Judgement Day because numerous believers have become disillusioned with the organized church and have slipped into a backslidden state.

Micah talked to the leaders of the people about the importance of *justice*. This is one of the themes which run throughout this chapter. The prophet asks, 'Should you [the leaders] not know justice?' (3:1). He went on to tell the people that he himself was 'filled with power, with the Spirit of the Lord, and with justice and might', and he warned them about false leaders who 'despise justice' (3:8, 9).

Our prophet paints a very clear picture of what these leaders were like. He told them, 'You ... hate good and love evil' (3:1). Amos had obviously had to deal with the same problem in the northern kingdom. He had exhorted his hearers to

'Seek good, not evil ...
Hate evil, love good;
maintain justice in the courts'   (Amos 5:14–15).

Isaiah too had declared,

'Stop doing wrong,
learn to do right!
Seek justice,
encourage the oppressed'   (Isaiah 1:16–17).

The need is still there today. Preachers should emphasize God's divine order. Christian people should stop reading, with sensual excitement, about die evil which wicked people are doing. Instead they should start applauding the good which is going on around them.

What were the leaders of Judah doing? They were behaving like butchers.[1] Micah used this description because the leaders were treating the ordinary people just like so much meat to be cut up and sold for profit. He said,

'You ... tear the skin from my people
and the flesh from their bones;
... [you] break their bones in pieces;
[and] chop them up like meat for the pan,
like flesh for the pot'   (3:2–3).

He meant that the people were being exploited by the very people who should be leading them into right ways.[2] They were being 'ripped off' left, right and centre. However, if any of these leaders were to stop to think about the consequences of their actions then, Micah tells them, they would discover that God had hidden his face from them. Listen to the solemn words with which Micah expresses this:

'Then they will cry out to the Lord,
but he will not answer them.
At that time he will hide his face from them
because of the evil they have done'   (3:4).

God does not forgive those who cry to him merely because
they are scared, and worried about their own position. He
cleanses the sins of those who truly repent and turn from their
evil way and trust in the Lord Jesus Christ alone for help and
salvation. Rather than hating good and loving evil, the people
should all 'hate what is evil [and] cling to what is good' (Romans
12:9).

The sins of the false prophets (3:5–8)
Again Micah begins with a statement (cf. 3:1). He says, 'This is
what the Lord says' (3:5). It is imperative that we should all take
notice of what God says. While everything that we need to know
for our salvation and our Christian life is written in the Bible,
we sometimes need people to spell out that message to us and
make it clear so that we are forced to take notice of it. That is
the task of a preacher. However, just as there were false prophets
and true prophets in Micah's day, so there are both false teachers
and faithful preachers in our own day. Every one of God's people
should make sure that they are 'sitting under' the teaching of
those who are true to God's Word.

Micah condemned certain prophets. He said, '[They] lead
my people astray' and 'They proclaim peace.' So how can we
tell the difference between a false teacher and a true one? We
have already seen Micah, a true prophet of the Lord, give his
credentials in verse 8 of this chapter. But this knowledge did not
cause him to be puffed up with conceit. He did not have to go
and stand in front of his audience or climb up onto a platform
in order to display his credentials for everyone to see. He had
the same humble attitude as Paul, who declared, 'The gift of

God's grace [was] given me through the working of his power. Although I am less than the least of God's people ...' (Ephesians 3:7-8). Micah was guided in what he said, not by the money that he was given, nor even by the needs of the people, but by the Spirit of the Lord.

Secondly, he said that his concern was that justice should be exercised. He would not be swayed by anyone or anything other than a burning desire that right should be done, and wrong should be condemned. And, like all true prophets of God, he was prepared to suffer for being faithful in declaring that message. Matthew Henry writes, 'Those who are sure that they have a commission from God need not be afraid of opposition from men.'[3] However, it is not enough to preach platitudes, even when they are true. 'Unless one declares the things a people needs need to know, and unless he condemns the sins of which they are guilty he is as much a false prophet as one who declares untruths or that which contradict truth.'[4]

The false prophets had to be condemned. They were, after all, leading God's people astray. They were encouraging the people to go in ways which were wrong. The book of Proverbs tells us, 'There is a way that seems right to a man, but in the end it leads to death' (Proverbs 14:12).

These false prophets were telling the inhabitants of Judah that everything was all right. Of course that was what they wanted to hear. We all love to hear good news. We long to be assured that everything is well. We desire an easy pathway through life. No wonder the people listened with pleasure when the false prophets said that everything was peaceful.

The message proclaimed by these men was similar to that of their counterparts in Jeremiah's day. Over a hundred years after Micah prophesied Jeremiah had to say of the false prophets,

'They dress the wound of my people
as though it were not serious.
"Peace, Peace," they say,
when there is no peace'   (Jeremiah 6:14).

Why did these prophets give their clients such false messages?
It was because they were paid well for giving them. That is
what Micah means by saying, 'If one feeds them they proclaim
"peace".' He puts it even more clearly later: 'Her prophets tell
fortunes for money' (3:11). The larger the sum paid for the
consultation, the more pleasant will be the prophecy. If someone
was unable to pay very much, then the prophet would 'prepare
to wage war against him' (3:5). Micah means that the poor client
will receive a terrible prediction regarding the future.

As Micah saw this kind of thing being done in the name of
religion it made him very distressed. He said that God would
judge these false prophets because what they were doing was
wrong (3:6-7). These people obviously did have some spiritual
power, as many who practise occult deeds have today, but the
powers they have will be taken away from them: 'The sun will
set for the prophets' (3:6). Instead of visions and divinations they
will only see darkness because night will come over them.

In addition, God will not answer their cry. The seers will be
ashamed because they will no longer be able to see into the
future. The diviners will be disgraced because they have only
used their powers to earn huge sums of money for themselves.
They will be like the prophets of Baal in Elijah's day who
shouted, 'O Baal, answer us!' 'But', said the writer of the Holy
Scriptures, 'There was no response; no one answered' (1 Kings
18:26). The consequences of the failure to serve the Lord were
that they were all seized and slaughtered in the Kishon Valley
(1 Kings 18:40).

The sins of responsible people (3:9–12)

Micah addressed all of the leaders of the land. He spoke to Jacob (the southern kingdom) and Israel (the northern kingdom). His message to them was that they all 'despise justice and distort all that is right' (3:9). He had been saying that all through this chapter, and especially in verses 1–3.

Next Micah cast his gaze over all the new buildings which were going up all over the city of Jerusalem. This was supposed to be the holy city. It had within it the temple, and the people had been hypnotized into a false sense of security by repeating, 'This is the temple of the Lord, the temple of the Lord, the temple of the Lord!' (Jeremiah 7:4). One of the things which made them confident was the fact that inside the temple stood the ark which, they thought, was a sure token of God's presence with his people.

But Micah did not spend time admiring all the fine, new buildings which had been erected in Jerusalem. Instead he said that these leaders had built Zion with bloodshed, and Jerusalem with wickedness (3:10). Undoubtedly the city had been built through immoral means. The people had sweated blood in putting up these buildings. Jeremiah was to say to King Jehoakim a century or so later:

'Woe to him who builds his palace by unrighteousness ...
making his countrymen work for nothing,
not paying them for their labour'   (Jeremiah 22:13).

It seems that the same kind of thing had happened in Micah's day[5]

This is how the system worked. The 'leaders judge for a bribe' (3:11). If people had a legal problem they went to a judge. If they could afford to pay the judge sufficient money, then he would find in their favour. This system must have been widespread because the writer of die Proverbs said, 'A wicked man accepts a bribe in secret to pervert the course of justice' (Proverbs 17:23). However, not only did these judges often 'acquit the guilty for a bribe', they regularly denied 'justice to the innocent' (Isaiah 5:23). How was that? It was because those people were too poor to give the judge any money. In fact, the poor often found that the court made no time to hear the cases of orphans or widows. (This practice was also condemned in Isaiah 1:23.)

Although I would not suggest that justice is wrought only on behalf of the rich in these days, it does seem that if the best lawyer cannot be afforded then an ordinary person does not stand such a good chance of winning his case as those who can pay the fees of the country's top advocates. When people from our church objected to a betting office being opened in our local shopping parade we lost the case. Our side was put by one of the elders from our church who, although he is a retired civil servant, had no training in the conduct of lawcourts. The other side was conducted by the country's leading expert in the field of betting law. We cannot help wondering whether the outcome would have been different had we been the ones who had hired the well-known lawyer and the bookmaker had put forward his own case.

Next Micah deals with the priests. He said that they 'teach for a price' (3:11). Rather than making a stand for justice and righteousness, the priests were only really interested in helping those who could afford to pay them a large sum of money for their advice. Today certain evangelists, particularly in the USA, can earn large sums of money for their religious 'performances' in front of television cameras. And in Britain a few popular authors charge large fees to speak at Christian gatherings. Is this really how preachers of God's Word ought to behave?

Finally, Micah said that the 'prophets tell fortunes for money'

(3:11). No one should be a Christian leader, or teacher, just to gain money for himself. It is right that those in positions of leadership should be paid fairly, or even generously. Jesus himself said, 'The worker deserves his wages' (Luke 10:7). But no one should use the service of God to make a fortune. The love of money is still 'a root of all kinds of evil' (1 Timothy 6:10).

Yet even though Micah often spoke up on behalf of the ordinary people, they still did not receive his message. They said things like this: 'We know that Micah is wrong in spreading all this doom and gloom because the Lord is certainly among us. We have the city of Jerusalem. We have the temple in our midst and we have the ark within the temple. No disaster will come upon us. We are the people of God. Jerusalem is the holy city. Doesn't the psalmist say, "The city ... [is] the holy place where the Most High dwells. God is within her, she will not fall"? (Psalm 46:4-5).'

What was God's answer to this kind of talk? The Lord said,

'Zion will be ploughed like a field,
Jerusalem will become a heap of rubble,
the temple hill a mound overgrown with thickets'   (3:12).

History tells us that something over a hundred years later this did happen. Jerusalem was totally destroyed.

The reason that the judgement foretold by Micah was delayed was because the people seemed to have repented and God, therefore, withheld his hand at that time. Likewise judgement eventually fell upon Nineveh, but it was not until 150 years later, because the people repented in the days of Jonah.

Micah pointed out in these verses that 'It is because of you that this terrible disaster will come upon the city' (3:12). A century later some elders in Jerusalem quoted Micah's words to those who wanted to murder Jeremiah. They said, 'No one put Micah to death for saying this. In fact, didn't King Hezekiah fear the Lord and seek his favour?' (see Jeremiah 26:18-19).

So, it seems that some, at least, did take notice of Micah's words. We know that a great reformation took place in the land at about that time (see 2 Kings 18:5-6) and Micah's efforts probably played a large part in the revival of true religion.

Some questions for us

As we contemplate this chapter we need to ask ourselves if we exercise any responsibility among the people of God. If we do not, then why is that the case? Have we no gifts, or are we too shy or too lazy to use them? It may be that God's work is being held back because his people are content to sit comfortably in their seats while others work extremely hard.

Those of us in positions of leadership need to ask, 'Am I being true to the Word of God?' Do I teach the truth of God whether I feel like it or not? (2 Timothy 4:2). Do I keep back anything for fear that it may give offence to people?

God's Word is as true today as it was in Micah's day. He will bring judgement upon sin and he will use any means to bring his people back into his ways.

5

The city of God

Please read Micah 4:1–13

God's people should not be preoccupied with all the terrible things which are going on round about them. When I was a boy, just after the Second World War, I often remember hearing my mother say to other people, 'It's not right to be bringing up children in a world like this.' The reason she was so apprehensive was because, although Hitler's army had been defeated and Japan had surrendered, the cold war had begun and the USSR and the USA were both experimenting with nuclear explosions. Everyone knew that if some crazy politician in Washington or Moscow pressed the wrong button a nuclear war could be started which could end up with the destruction of all civilization in a matter of minutes.

Fear of nuclear war was not the only thing that worried people in those days. Because of the austerity measures being taken, everything was in short supply. There seemed to be little to be cheerful about. For several years things looked very black.

However, better times did come, and few people disputed the words of the prime minister, Harold MacMillan, when he said, 'You've never had it so good.' Materially, life was much improved.

When we think back to those fearful days of the late 1950s and early 1960s we get a vague idea of what it may have been like for the people of Judah during the time when Micah preached. The people of the southern kingdom had the constant threat of mighty Assyria hanging over them. They were looking for some message of hope, some news that things were going to improve. But instead they heard Micah say, 'Jerusalem [the city of God] will become a heap of rubble, the temple hill a mound overgrown with thickets' (3:12). They must have been devastated when they heard these words spoken by God's prophet.

The destiny of the city (4:1-5)
However, at the beginning of chapter 4 of Micah we discover that there is a sudden and dramatic change from the gloom written about at the end of chapter 3. The prophet told his audience what was going to happen in the last days. When we read the words, 'the last days', in prophecy they are usually referring to that period of time between the first coming of Christ and his second coming. These are the days which include the twentieth century.

The prophets were not so much men who predicted the future (as though they were looking into a crystal ball) as those who burned with messages from God which were aimed directly at the people of their day. However, these prophecies also had many implications for times far beyond their own—especially in relation to God's people and the coming deliverer, the Messiah. When the prophets looked into the future it was as though they were gazing at range upon range of mountains stretching away into the distance. And, as we read their prophecies, it is not easy to distinguish between those prophecies which refer especially to New Testament times, and those which are yet to be fulfilled. In other words, many prophecies have different perspectives. They refer to the prophet's own times, to the gospel age, the glories of the Second Coming of Christ and the days of eternity.

We can imagine Micah, as he prophesied, lifting his gaze upwards as he looked far into the future. He had been absolutely correct in saying that Jerusalem would be destroyed; just over a century later the Babylonians did utterly demolish the whole city, including the temple. However, the temple did not remain as a ruin; it was rebuilt at the time of Haggai and some centuries later it was 'improved' by Herod the Great. Later still the baby Jesus was circumcised in its courts. Then, at the age of twelve, Christ was dedicated to the Lord within its precincts. And finally, the Lord Jesus Christ came into Jerusalem, first of all in triumph (on what is called Palm Sunday) and then to be arrested and mocked. It was at that time that the Lord rejected the temple because the people turned their backs upon him and said, 'We will not have this man to reign over us' (Luke 19:14, AV).

So, if the Lord himself rejected the temple, and all of its religious ritual, why does Micah speak in such glowing terms of it here in chapter 4? It is because he is speaking, not of the literal Jerusalem and Mount Zion (which is still there in Israel underneath two large Muslim mosques), but of a better mountain and a more holy temple. He declares that this mountain of the Lord's temple will be established; he is certain of it.

What does he mean by 'the mountain of the Lord's temple'? To find the answer we have to go to the New Testament. The apostle Paul, writing to the church at Corinth, said, 'Don't you know that you yourselves are God's temple and that God's Spirit lives in you? If anyone destroys God's temple, God will destroy him; for God's temple is sacred, and *you are that temple*' (1 Corinthians 3:16–17).

In other words, the church is now God's temple. By 'the church' I do not mean any particular denomination or Christian organization (the Bible never uses the word 'church' in either of those senses). I mean the whole company of God's own blood-bought people. Here, Micah is looking beyond the Jewish religion and beyond the cross. He is looking far ahead (in verses 1–5). So let us examine what Micah says about the church both in our days and in eternity (see Revelation 21).

He says mat the church of Jesus Christ is exalted far above all things:

> 'In the last days
> the mountain of the Lord's temple will be established
> as chief among the mountains;
> it will be raised above the hills,
> and peoples will stream to it'   (4:1).

No other religion is to be compared with true Christianity. The Lord Jesus Christ said that he is the only way to God. These are his words: 'I am the way and the truth and the life.' Then he adds, 'No one comes to the Father except through me' (John 14:6). How foolish it is, then, for 'the church' to hold multi-faith services, because all those who seek God through any means other than by faith in the Lord Jesus Christ alone are deluded. There is no other way to God. 'Salvation is found in no one else, for there is no other name under heaven given to men by which we must be saved' (Acts 4:12).

However, this does not mean that we should not want to speak to Muslims, Jews and Hindu people. But there is a vast difference in being friendly towards them, and people of other religions, and sharing worship with them. We should never ignore our neighbours who practise a false religion. On the contrary, we should do everything in our power to witness to them about the uniqueness of the Lord Jesus Christ, the only Saviour from sin.

So, we can see from these opening verses something about God's plan for his church. Next Micah says, 'Peoples will stream to it' (i.e. the church will grow in numbers).

'Many nations will come and say,
"Come let us go up to the mountain of the Lord,
to the house of the God of Jacob"'   (4:2).

Psalm 46 gives us the same picture of God in the midst of his city (his church). In verse 4 of that psalm we read, 'There is a river whose streams make glad the city of God,' and Micah takes up this theme, saying that this stream is made up of many nations. It refreshes the city of God. Even more wonderful, it is a stream which flows uphill! And it contains huge numbers of people from many nations. John tells us in Revelation, 'After this I looked and there before me was a great multitude that no one could count, from every nation, tribe, people and language, standing before the throne and in front of the Lamb' (Revelation 7:9). This same image is found in the prophecy of Micah. The phrases 'many peoples' and 'nations' are found in Micah chapter 4, in verses 1, 2, 3 (three times) and 5. This has relevance to the days in which we live, but it also refers to the glories of the last days (i.e., the times of heavenly glory when Christ will reign, unchallenged, over all).

We can gain a small glimpse of the meaning of this passage when we meet for worship with people from all kinds of nations worshipping God together in the same church. In Hania, on the lovely Greek island of Crete, my family once worshipped in an international church where there were many languages spoken. But we all praised God together. Of course, there can be a few problems when everyone speaks different languages, but there is a simple solution to that problem (at least from a lazy Englishman's point of view): let them all speak, or understand English! This, in fact, is what often happens in international services.

A third thing that we can learn about the church from this chapter is that God is going to teach the people in his church. In verse 2 we read,

"'He will teach us his ways,
so that we may walk in his paths."
The law will go out from Zion,
the word of the Lord from Jerusalem'   (4:2).

That is one of the reasons why people should go to church. They ought to want to be taught the ways of the Lord so that they can walk in his paths (i.e., obey him). Each of us needs to ask ourselves, 'Do I want to be instructed in the things of God?' If I do, then I should make sure that what I am paying attention to is indeed the Word of God. God himself speaks today through his servants, but only when they are faithful to die inerrant Word of God—the Bible (cf. 3:5-7, 8). We should all beware of listening to men's ideas which are not firmly based on the Scriptures.

Next we see that God will dispense justice in his church. We read, 'He will judge between many peoples and will settle disputes for strong nations far and wide' (4:3). Again we have a clear picture of God's deliverer (the Messiah) bringing peace.

These things which are outlined by Micah presented a great contrast to what went on in those days. In chapter 3:9 we read that me leaders of the people despised justice and distorted all that is right. But that was not God's way of doing things. He says that righteousness will prevail within me kingdom of God. God is just in all his actions. He does not overlook me iniquity of his people. That is why he had to send his own Son to die. It was to take upon himself me punishment that was due because of his people's sin.

Because of God's just ways, there is a time coming when war will be no more, and me weapons of mass destruction will be turned into implements fashioned for peace and prosperity. At that time Micah says,

'They will beat their swords into ploughshares
and their spears into pruning hooks.
Nation will not take up sword against nation,
nor will they train for war any more'   (4:3).

However, the prophet Joel spoke of the opposite thing happening, but this was because he was writing about a time when the enemies of God would be judged and destroyed. He said, 'Beat your ploughshares into swords and your pruning hooks into spears' (Joel 3:10). Isaiah, on the other hand, joins with Micah in speaking about the great days of universal peace and prosperity which will come upon all of the people of God (Isaiah 2:4). In fact, Isaiah 2:2-5 is almost identical to the words Micah uses in this passage, although Isaiah uses them in a different context from Micah.

There has been much written about whether Micah quoted from what Isaiah had already written, or vice versa; or whether they both cited an older, and well-known prophecy. Hengstenberg concludes that Isaiah copied from Micah[1] and Fairbairn agrees. He says, 'There are pretty strong grounds for the conclusion that it appeared first in the prophecies of Micah.'[2] But Alec Motyer believes that 'A comparison of the two texts weighs heavily in favour of an Isaianic origin.'[3] Whatever the case, the burden of these words appears in both of these important prophecies and they must not be ignored.

Another aspect of the church that Micah tells us about is that God will grant peace to his people. He says,

'Every man will sit under his own vine
and under his own fig-tree,
and no one will make them afraid,
for the Lord Almighty has spoken'   (4:4).

We do not yet enjoy these times, but in a spiritual sense we can experience the peace of God, which transcends all understanding, guarding our hearts and minds in Christ Jesus (Philippians 4:7). Those who truly belong to the Lord know that deep-down peace always, despite the outward trials that they may be passing through at any time.

The promise for all believers is that mere will come a day when a period of tranquillity will exist in every place. Then 'Every man will sit under his own vine and under his own fig-tree.' This is a figure which is often used to symbolize peace and prosperity (e.g., 1 Kings 4:25; Zechariah 3:10). The spreading vine and the large leaves of the fig-tree provide wonderful shade in hot Mediterranean lands.

Our family have often sat under the grapevines which hang down over the forecourts of tavernas in Greece, enjoying the shade and coolness which are always provided by these broad-leaved spreading plants. But here the prophet is not speaking of the benefit of sheltering under trees belonging to other people; he speaks about the time when every man will sit under his *own* plant. He will not be taking refuge, as a hunted man, under anyone else's vine or fig-tree. He will not be afraid, because the Lord Almighty has spoken; he has uttered his words of peace which go right into the soul of his own child.

Lastly, God's people will be constant in their love for him:

'All the nations may walk
in the name of their gods;
we will walk in the name of the Lord
our God for ever and ever'   (4:5).

Other people may be foolish enough to persist in their false religions, but God's people confess, love, obey and rely on the Lord for ever. 'Their witness will shine all the brighter amid the darkness around them.'[4] Peter wrote, 'since everything will be destroyed ... what kind of people ought you to be? You ought to live holy and godly lives as you look forward to the day of God' (2 Peter 3:11–12).

Let us have this resolve: 'We will walk in the name of the Lord our God for ever and ever'. 'In history there was only one who "walked in the name of the Lord for ever" and that was Christ himself.'[5] But there is a day coming when we shall be for ever with the Lord in that blessed land of peace and prosperity which is called heaven. Then we shall be free from the sin and disquiet of this life of sorrow and pain.

God's plan for the city (4:6–13)
Micah once again starts this section in a similar way, with the phrase, 'In that day ...' He is still speaking to the people about that time which is yet in the future—the period after the atoning death of the Lord Jesus Christ on the cross has taken place. However, he uses language which the people of his day would understand. He speaks of the 'lame', the 'exiles', those who have experienced 'grief', 'a remnant' and 'a strong nation'.

At the time when Micah was speaking, the people of Judah were surrounded by the invading army of the Assyrians. This would have made them feel lame in their attempts to fight off the aggressors. They knew that the peoples conquered by this nation were often taken away as captives, into exile, but worse still was happening. The Assyrians were not the only enemies of the people of the southern kingdom; there were many other strong nations who were opposing them as well.

It was not surprising that Micah's hearers saw themselves as being in a hopeless situation. However, that is not how God saw it. He said,

'I will gather the lame;
I will assemble the exiles
and those I have brought to grief.
I will make the lame a remnant,
those driven away a strong nation'   (4:6–7).

The Lord spoke to them most emphatically; he kept saying 'I will.'

It must have been a great comfort for the people of Judah to hear such things said concerning their future. However, the Lord God Almighty not only promised to do these things for them; he actually had the power to do all that he purposed. Furthermore, he not only said that he would deliver them as individuals; he told them that he would restore them as a nation once again. The people of Judah had often experienced grief in their history but, as other prophets had also said, they still had among them those who were faithful to the Lord. This group of people were described as being a remnant of their nation and they were the lame ones to whom these promises were made.

Micah then addressed the 'watchtower of the flock' (4:8). By that he meant the city of Jerusalem, the city which stood proudly on a hill. That city had for many years provided a site from which the surrounding area could be watched for wild animals and sheep-stealers. It had been a stronghold of the Daughter of Zion (the people of God), but in the days of Micah it was cowering, almost defeated, at the threat of the Assyrian army which was at its doorstep.

This is the burden of Micah's message at this point: 'Everything will be all right once again one day.' He was not like the many false prophets of that day who were telling the people of Jerusalem that there would be an immediate peace. Micah makes it clear that their former dominion would be restored to them at some time in the future. He meant that strong, permanent kingship would come once again to the city and people of Jerusalem.

We have here a picture of a shepherd and a king. In the ancient world kingship was often associated with the idea of a shepherd of the people.[6] David was a shepherd who transferred the skills which he had learned in his former occupation to his new role as king so that he could rule the people well. For believers today it is the Lord Jesus Christ who is their King, and the Lord's people are subjects in the kingdom of God; King Jesus is called 'the Good Shepherd'. So, despite all the fears of Judah then, and those of God's people today, everything will be well, one day, for those who commit all their ways to the Lord.

However, before these great things can be accomplished the nation must go through a period of great pain. Even good King Hezekiah was proving ineffective at that time. He had been the means of bringing people back to the ways of God (see 2 Kings 18) but things had become worse, rather than better. The effect of his poor rule had left the people in great anguish. This is why Micah spoke very plainly to them:

'Why do you now cry aloud—
have you no king?
Has your counsellor perished,
that pain seizes you like that of a woman in labour,

for now you must leave the city
to camp in the open field.
You will go to Babylon;
there you will be rescued.
There the Lord will redeem you
out of the hand of your enemies'   (4:9–10).

The prophet told them that they would become captives. It will be no good for them at that time to cry to the Lord and say, 'But we have returned to you. Will you still bring great trouble upon us?' The exile is going to take place because it is God's plan that it should.

It is often those who live closest to the Lord who are called upon to go through the most difficult experiences in life. It must have been very hard for the people to hear that they were going to have to leave their beloved city and camp in the open field. What indignity that would be for a citizen of Jerusalem to have to undergo!

Yet the strange thing is that God tells them, not that they will go to Assyria (the country which was threatening them at that time), but that they will be taken to Babylon. This must have been a great puzzle to the people. What was the significance of Babylon? Babylon was a comparatively feeble power at that time. But when God said this, through his servant Micah, he was looking a long way into the future (he is the God of the past, present and future). The Lord knew that over a hundred years later it would be Babylon who would be the dominant kingdom in that part of the world. Babylon would arise and carry out the purposes of God by punishing the people of the southern kingdom. This was the disaster which he had spoken of in Micah 2:3.

Good news

However, at the same time as news of judgement upon Judah was being given, there also came a word concerning deliverance. Micah tells them,

> 'There [in Babylon] you will be rescued.
> There [in Babylon] the Lord will redeem you
> out of the hand of your enemies'   (4:10).

It is often when things are at their blackest that the Lord at last reaches into our situation and grants us salvation. The psalmist tells us that 'A righteous man may have many troubles, but the Lord delivers him from them all' (Psalm 34:19). In the dark days of famine Elijah was sent to Zarephath to stay with a poor widow. When the prophet came she was gathering a few sticks to make a fire on which to cook a final meal for her son and herself before they both died of starvation. It was then that God said to Elijah, 'I have commanded a widow *in that place* to supply you with food' (1 Kings 17:9). And, strange as it may seem to us, the sustenance of Elijah came through that poor widow, who, to all intents and purposes, was about to die. Micah is saying to Judah that the same kind of thing would happen to them. It would be there, in the dreadful land of captivity, that the Lord would save his people.

Following this word of cheer, Micah brought his hearers back to the present time with a bump. He said, 'But now many nations are gathered against you' (4:11). These invaders were going to gloat over the people of Judah. But, before they could give up in despair Micah said, 'They do not know the thoughts of the Lord; they do not understand his plan' (4:12). Those who are enemies of God and his people often seem to be winning the battle. However, they do not know the plan of the Lord— and he does have one. Later on God spoke through the prophet Jeremiah: 'I know the plans I have for you ... plans to prosper

you and not to harm you, plans to give you a hope and a future'
(Jeremiah 29:11).

Micah went on to tell his audience that God would cause his
own people to rise up against the heathen nations and dash
them to pieces. The ill-gotten gains which the Assyrians had
taken from Judah would be taken from them and restored once
again to the Lord and his people. Sennacherib, the Assyrian king,
called himself, 'king over the world'[7] but it will be the God of the
people of Jerusalem who will show himself to be 'the Lord of all
the earth' (4:13).

So those of us who are fearful of what the future holds need
to remember these things: the Lord's name will be upheld,
despite all the attacks of the evil one. God's people, even though
they might be in a place of darkness, where God does not seem
to be answering their prayers, will be delivered. The enemy of
God does seem to be winning the battle, 'but they do not know
the thoughts of the Lord; they do not understand his plan' (4:12).
We need always to keep in mind that the Lord God Almighty
will rescue and redeem those of us who belong to him and grant
us rest and peace. He will do this for us because we trust in the
Lord Jesus Christ alone for our salvation.

There is a chorus which I used to sing, long ago in Sunday
School days, which sums up this thought:

O the love which drew salvation's plan,
O the grace that brought it down to man
O the mighty guilt which God did span
At Calvary.

Mercy there was great and grace was free,
Pardon there was multiplied to me;
There my burdened soul found liberty,
At Calvary.[8]

God's gracious promises

Please read Micah 5:1–15

In the middle of a great deal of talk concerning the oppression being brought about by Judah's enemies, and judgement upon sin, we read some very familiar words (5:2). This is the prophecy which was found by the religious people of Herod's household when the Magi came to King Herod and asked, 'Where is the one who has been born king of the Jews? We saw his star in the east and have come to worship him' (Matthew 2:2). The passage that the teachers of the law had looked up was Micah 5:2. From this we learn that the name of the town where Jesus was to be born was called Bethlehem Ephrathah.

God's deliverer (5:1–6)

However, it was not only Herod's household which was greatly troubled at the question asked by the Magi; many hundreds of years earlier all of the inhabitants of Jerusalem, and all of Judah, were also filled with anxiety. This was because the Assyrian army had, some time before, deported the northern kingdom and, at the time when Micah wrote this, they were right at the gates of the capital city (1:9). This explains why Micah called upon the people to be ready. They would not be able to protect themselves if they were lethargic, choosing to wait and see what was going to happen when the invading army arrived. Action was called for, and pretty quickly too.

Micah called Jerusalem the 'city of troops'. All of its citizens had to be called up and set to work in the defence of the city. That is why Micah calls out, 'Marshal your troops ... for a siege is laid against us' (5:1). Even though they were to do this, things were not going to go well for them. Micah tells the people that Israel's ruler is going to be insulted. This is what he meant when he said, 'They will strike Israel's ruler on the cheek with a rod' (5:1).

This would be a dreadful thing to happen to the king of any country, but this king was the ruler of Judah, God's nation. The Lord Jesus Christ was treated like that. On the night when he was arrested, and was awaiting the outcome of his various trials, the Roman soldiers taunted him (Luke 22:64). We find it difficult to even think about, but the Lord Jesus Christ was greatly humiliated on that occasion. The soldiers dressed him in purple and then they did what was prophesied about Israel's ruler: they struck him about the face.

There are also other occasions in the Bible when it is recorded that godly people were struck in the face. Zedekiah slapped the prophet Micaiah in the face and taunted him by saying, 'Which way did the spirit from the Lord go when he went from me to speak to you?' (1 Kings 22:24). Job said that men jeered at him and struck his cheek in scorn (Job 16:10) and Paul, writing to the Corinthians, makes reference to a slap in the face (2 Corinthians 11:20).[1]

Some time later, when great sieges were laid against Jerusalem, Micah's prophecy was fulfilled. Zedekiah, the last king of Judah, who had been blinded, was taken away into Babylon (2 Kings 25:7). We can imagine what dreadful things probably happened to him when we read about some of the cruel practices of the Assyrians and Babylonians which are told us in our history books.

Why were the Assyrians now at the gate of the city of Jerusalem? Their plan was to capture the seat of government. They would then be in a position to conquer and rule over the whole land of Israel. But their plans did not come to fruition because the Lord had other plans (see 2:3). His design was that, from the city of Bethlehem, would come a powerful one who would be given to the people of God to rule over them.

Bethlehem lay just a few miles to the south-east of Jerusalem. It was only a small, rather insignificant place, but it had this claim to fame: it was the birthplace of the great King David, the one who had unified the land and had gone down in history as the powerful deliverer of the land and its people. So, through Micah, God gave this promise:

'But you, Bethlehem Ephrathah,
though you are small among the clans of Judah,
out of you will come for me
one who will be ruler over Israel'   (5:2).

The person who was going to arise would be ruler over the whole land and people. To hear such certainties spoken of was just what the people most needed in those days of fear and uncertainty. Moreover, the promised deliverer was going to come, not just for the benefit of the people of Judah, but, said the Lord, 'He is going to come *for me!*' He would be the servant of the Lord. In other words, he was going to be a great and powerful king who would rule over the entire nation.

Then Micah added some further words of explanation: 'whose origins are from of old, from ancient times'. Proverbs 8:23 uses the same kind of words: 'I was appointed from eternity, from the beginning, before the world began.' So, for the believer, there is no doubt about the identity of this person. There is only one man who has existed from all eternity, and that is the Lord Jesus Christ.

Micah said that this coming ruler is the one who 'will stand and shepherd his flock in the strength of the Lord, in the majesty of the name of the Lord his God' (5:4). He is going to be the Shepherd/King who will restore the kingdom (see 4:8). When he comes the people of God 'will live securely, for then his greatness will reach to the ends of the earth. And he will be their peace' (5:4–5).

Those who have the assurance that their sins have been forgiven, and who have dedicated their lives to the service of the Lord, experience many spiritual blessings. They know security from all their fears, and they are aware of the peace of God in every area of their lives. Isaiah calls this ruler 'the Prince of Peace' (Isaiah 9:6) and Paul looks upon him as 'our peace' (Ephesians 2:14).

We see in this passage a very clear picture of the Lord Jesus Christ, our Shepherd and our King. However, there is another meaning here as well. Micah tells us that this ruler is coming for the benefit of his faithful people, but there is a further reference to the Jewish captivity in Babylon (4:10). In verse 3 we read about Israel being 'abandoned until the time when she who is in labour gives birth'. This is a figure of the remnant of God's people, 'the rest of his brothers,' returning to join the family of Israel.[2]

The Lord Jesus Christ was born of a woman, Mary, who experienced birth-pangs at Bethlehem some 700 years after this prophecy was given. Micah's contemporary, Isaiah, takes up the same prophetic strands, but he refers to a nation being brought forth in a moment (Isaiah 66:8). There 'The pregnant mother figure gives birth, not to a child, but to a nation ... The apostles on the Day of Pentecost must have thought of this one as they witnessed thousands turning to Christ.'[3]

Furthermore, the Lord Jesus Christ will bring about reconciliation between people. He will shepherd (care for and meet every need of) his flock because they are his own blood-bought people. He will grant them security and he will give them his peace. These are all blessings of the gospel which have been purchased for each believer through the atoning death of the Lord on the cross of Calvary.

A new section begins at the second sentence in verse 5. The prophet abruptly returns his hearers to their own time. All this talk of future peace and security must not allow them to forget about the danger which was then at their doors. Micah was a realist. He talked to them about the time 'when the Assyrian invades our land' (5:5). He told them that the enemy was going to march through their fortresses. This enemy was very powerful and Judah's defence system would not be strong enough to stop him. He would pass straight through the barriers which they had erected to hold him back. So, what could be done to halt this evil invader?

Micah reminds them of the words of God which are recorded in verse 1. They were to rise up against the invader. With the Lord on their side they would not be leaderless (despite the weakness of their king—4:9).

'When the Assyrian invades our land
and marches through our fortresses,
we will raise against him seven shepherds'   (5:5).

Seven is the perfect number and the Lord promises that he is going to be like seven marshals of the people. To make it even clearer Micah adds: 'even eight leaders of men'. In fact weak Judah is, under the power of the Lord, going to be so strong that, to their enemies, it would seem as if they have even more than the seven shepherds which had been promised to them.

God was saying that he would give them the power to drive these Assyrians from off their land. It will seem as if they, by their influence, will 'rule the land of Assyria with the sword, [and] the land of Nimrod [another name for Assyria] with drawn sword' (5:6). In fact, we know that this kind of thing did come to pass because, by the action of the Lord, the invading army departed and left Judah alone.

Micah then follows this statement up by telling the people of the actions of God. He says,

'He will deliver us from the Assyrian
when he invades our land
and marches into our borders'   (5:6).

God's remnant (5:7–9)
Micah gave two oracles about God's faithful remnant. The first one is written in verses 7–9, and the second in verses 10–15.

In the first oracle God's faithful ones are called 'the remnant of Jacob' (5:7, 8). Often the remnant of the people of God are said to belong to Jacob. Jacob was the rather weak younger twin of Esau, yet he gained the birthright from his stronger brother and became one of the great ancestors of the Israelites. The remnant spoken of here is said to be 'in the midst of many peoples' (5:7) and 'among the nations, in the midst of many peoples' (5:8). Although they are small in number and weak in power, God's purpose for them is that they will be a great witness to the surrounding nations.

The prophet said that there would be two aspects to their work. First, they will be 'like dew from the Lord, like showers on the grass, which do not wait for man or linger for mankind' (5:7). Those who live in hot countries know the value of dew, especially when it has not rained for a long while. It is the only refreshment to the parched land. So, Micah said, the remnant of the people were going to bring great refreshment to the nations who were feeling parched and dry—just as we, today, should be a great blessing to the people who live round about us as we bring them the good news of the gospel of salvation through the Lord Jesus Christ, whose death brings atonement for repentant sinners. Peter and John told their congregation about Christ. They said, 'Repent ... and turn to God so that your sins may be wiped out, that times of refreshing may come from the Lord' (Acts 3:19). The faithful remnant of God's people will have the glorious task of bringing wonderful news of blessing to the people of the world who turn to God in faith.

But the second aspect of the people's witness would be to tell of judgement upon sin and sinners. This is what Micah means when he declares that God's remnant will be 'like a lion among the beasts of the forest, like a young lion among flocks of sheep, which mauls and mangles as it goes, and no one can rescue' (5:8). Why did the prophet give this terrible sign? He spoke like this because he wanted to bring them to repentance.

There are some people who are wooed into the kingdom of God by the gracious entreaties of the Lord, but others are frightened into the kingdom because they are convicted of the enormity of their sin against God, who is holy. The reason they flee to Christ for salvation is because they are afraid of the eternal punishment which is due to them because of their sin. Whichever way people are spoken to, they must make sure that they come to the Lord Jesus Christ, seeking the deliverance which only he can bring; his salvation is complete and lasting.

Micah then encourages God's people in their witness. He says, 'Your hand will be lifted up in triumph over your enemies and all your foes will be destroyed' (5:9). This is a very strong word. God does not say that the Assyrians will be frightened off. He says that they will be destroyed, as the entire army of Egyptians which had followed the Israelites into the sea were all drowned so that not one of them survived (Exodus 14:28).

The Lord was going to do all this through the instrumentality of weak Judah. She would discover the power of the Lord working through her. She would realize, with Paul, the truth that 'When I am weak, then I am strong' (2 Corinthians 12:10). Many saints can testify that when they hand over their fears and frailty to the Lord then they receive great strength to do his work. He grants them the power of the Holy Spirit, who makes them 'more than conquerors' (Romans 8:37).

God's destruction (5:10–15)
This section details many of the things that the Lord 'will do'. Micah said that God was going to do great things through the faithful remnant of his people. However, this ability was not going to come to them automatically, merely because they were following the Lord. They were going to have to trust in God alone to be able to do their work. All the things on which the people of Judah had formerly relied would be wrenched away from them. God is a jealous God and he will share the hearts of his people with nothing and no one. Therefore, Micah made this bold declaration that Judah was going to be cleansed. All the things which they had been leaning on would prove to be

inadequate; they were going to be removed. God is going to do a great deal of destroying. Four times he said, 'I will destroy' (5:10, 11, 12, 13). Then in verse 14 he changed it to, 'I will uproot' and in verse 15 he declares, 'I will take vengeance.'

What was it that God was going to remove from the people? He said that he would destroy their horses (5:10). These animals were their main means of war. If their horses were going to be destroyed then they would have no need of chariots either.

They depended for the defence of their land upon the armaments of their day, but if they were going to serve God faithfully, they were going to have to trust only in God, who had promised to be their defence and shield. Psalm 20:7 states, 'Some trust in chariots and some in horses, but we trust in the name of the Lord our God.' This was going to have to be the attitude of Judah.

Next the Lord says, 'I will destroy the cities of your land and tear down all your strongholds' (5:11). He is talking about fortified cities here. In the year 701 BC Micah's words came true: Nebuchadnezzar conquered the city of Jerusalem itself and utterly destroyed it.

He is a foolish person who puts his whole faith in walled cities. The message is that only those who rely on God will be kept secure from their enemies.

God then said,

'I will destroy your witchcraft
and you will no longer cast spells.
I will destroy your carved images
and your sacred stones from among you;
you will no longer bow down
to the work of your hands'   (5:12–13).

It is a very foolish nation who trusts witchcraft. That people can never be safe because all of these things come from the devil. Hallowe'en celebrations may seem harmless fun but those who indulge in the ancient activities connected with that evening are potentially dabbling in witchcraft.

If Judah was going to know the strength of the Lord then she was going to have to turn her back upon all of these dangerous practices. Only God can tell the future. Only he can guide people into right paths.

Finally, through Micah, the Lord speaks of Judah's hankering back to Canaanite religious practices. He said, 'I will uproot from among you your Asherah poles and demolish your cities' (5:14). According to 2 Kings 18:4, Hezekiah ordered the destruction of all of these sacred symbols but it seems that the people were still harking back to them. This sin is condemned in the very first of the Ten Commandments, which says, 'You shall have no other gods before me' (Exodus 20:3). Despite this clear statement by the Lord, the people of God were wanting to prostitute themselves before other (false) religions. In doing so they were being unfaithful to God, their Lover and their Lord (see Isaiah 54:5).

Then, and not until these things have been completely dealt with, will the Lord smite the heathen nations who were plaguing Judah. When God's people have obeyed the Lord, then God will turn in vengeance upon their enemies. He said, 'I will take vengeance in anger and wrath upon the nations that have not obeyed me' (5:15). The Lord is angry with the nations who have not obeyed him. He will be just as angry with any individual who disobeys his command to come unto him and find rest for his or her soul (Matt 11:28).

Some things to think about

There are many troubles all around us as I write in this last decade of the twentieth century, but the Lord has already sent his deliverer. The Lord Jesus Christ has come and he will deal with all the afflictions of true believers in the Lord Jesus Christ. We need to come to him for the salvation which he offers so freely to all repentant sinners.

God's people should be exercising the twofold ministry of telling of the sweet refreshing which God freely gives to those who come to him for redemption and warning sinners of the consequences of their evil ways (see Ezekiel 33:7-9). We each of us need to ask ourselves how diligent are we in the work of telling unbelievers about the Lord Jesus Christ who, alone, can save them from the guilt and power of their sin.

God requires that his people root out of their lives everything which comes between their trust in God and their own selfishness. Our desire should be that of William Cowper when he wrote,

The dearest idol I have known,
Whate'er that idol be;
Help me to tear it from thy throne
And worship only thee.[4]

When things have been put right between ourselves and the Lord, then, and only then, will we experience that real, lasting, satisfying peace in our souls which is spoken about in this passage.

7

The requirements of our holy God

Please read Micah 6:1-16

There often arise in our lives those times of crisis when we are perplexed. We find that we have a number of choices open to us, and we do not know which one to take. Sometimes the pressure upon us is very great and we become so anxious that we are almost in despair. In such circumstances we find it very difficult to work out what to do for the best. We know that whatever action we take, someone is going to get upset, or at the very least, feel that we have let him or her down. In the end (it is such a pity that we do not do it at the beginning)—in the end we cry out to the Lord, 'What do you want me to do?'

Micah 6 is about the behaviour of God's people in the face of all kinds of problems. It is summed up in the question: 'What does the Lord require of you?' (6:8). The same enquiry is addressed to every fellowship of God's people today. Churches should not be asking, 'What do *we* want?' or even, 'What should we do?' It is more definite than that. The question is: 'What does *the Lord* require of you?' It is what God demands from his people which matters more than anything else in the life of local Christian churches.

The Lord's charge (6:1–3)

Through Micah the Lord called the people to attention. He said, 'Listen' (6:1). To understand the implication of the word, 'listen', or 'hear', we need to remember that the people of Judah were in a terrible state. The dreaded Assyrian army was surrounding them on every side, and they were not an unknown quantity. The Judeans were aware of some of the awful things the heathen Assyrians had done to their northern neighbours. They must surely have thought that they too would shortly be captured and deported like the people of the northern kingdom, and many other nations, had been.

Some of us, who were alive in 1940, can remember the time when a few miles away over the English Channel, Hitler and his huge army were poised to invade our beloved country. I can recall how scared I felt, even though I was only five years old at the time. It seemed to our whole nation that a great black cloud hung very low over everything. The news each day appeared to be darker and more awesome. The terrible dread, which affected everyone, would just not go away.

The same kind of pressure must have been upon God's people in the days of Micah. Therefore, they must have been glad to learn that God was going to speak to them. After all, they were the covenant people of God and they knew that in the past the Lord had often delivered their nation from the hands of their foes. So now they eagerly waited to hear the voice of the Lord.

However, they must have been very surprised when the Lord did speak, because he made no allusion to the enemy outside; instead he spoke about the enemy within. God made no mention of the Assyrian enemy and their wickedness; his main concern was about the spiritual lifestyle of God's people.[1]

When we are in trouble we are so quick to blame others. We are even tempted to think that the fault is God's, but, until we are forced to do so, we seldom look at our own condition. What a shock it must have been for the Judeans to hear Micah telling the people that 'The Lord has a case against his people; he is lodging a charge against Israel'! (6:2). Such a statement makes each company of God's people think about their relationship to God. Is the Lord saying that he has a case against the church today? Is the Holy Spirit prompting God's people as individuals to think about the things in their own lives which are wrong and need to be dealt with?

The scene in this chapter is a court of law. Lawcourts are very solemn and serious places, and the one depicted in this chapter is the most stern of all because it is God's court that we are looking into. The witnesses and the jury are the mountains which are all around Judah (whom he now calls by their covenant name, 'Israel'). These 'everlasting foundations of the earth' have witnessed everything that has happened to God's people right from the beginning of time. They were witnesses of the covenant which God made with Israel (Deuteronomy 32:1). They knew that Israel had solemnly promised to obey the commands of the Lord and, in return, God would bless them and make them his own special people. Now, as Micah permitted the people to observe the spectacle, the eternal mountains were waiting to hear the charge which the Lord was about to bring against Judah.

However, first of all, the Lord calls upon his people to speak in their own defence. We can almost hear the agony in his voice as he says to them, 'My people [the A.V. translates this, 'O my people'—see also Isaiah 5:4], what have I done to you? How have I burdened you?' Then, to emphasize his anguish, he calls out, 'Answer me.' But they do not answer, not one word. In any case, what could they say? They knew they were in the wrong. They had disobeyed the Lord's commands time and time again; and every time they confessed their sin and turned back to the Lord, he forgave them. Now once again he had caught them behaving in an openly sinful way. They could not answer the charge, because they knew they were guilty.

The Lord's case (6:4–5)

In these verses God used his prophet to point out to the people some of the ways in which he had blessed Israel in the past. He reminded them of all their years of slavery in Egypt. There they were in a helpless, hopeless condition. They were entirely in the grip of the cruel Egyptians, and they could do nothing to save themselves. However, the Lord had redeemed them, and brought them up from the land of bondage. It is not only in the book of Exodus that we read of this incident. Because it was such a powerful story of deliverance, it is related, or alluded to, in different parts of the Old Testament Scriptures on numerous occasions.

The picture of the children of Israel in slavery is a description of sinners without Christ. Once we were all slaves of Satan, fast bound in sin. But then God stooped down and lifted us up out of our iniquity and degradation and, through the atoning death of Christ on Calvary, he made us new men and women. It is always good for believers to look back to the time of their salvation and remember its joy. For many years believers have been singing the beautiful words of Charles Wesley:

My chains fell off, my heart was free,
I rose, went forth and followed thee.[2]

Secondly, God reminded the Israelites of the leaders he had raised up for them. Some of these were very godly people. The people would have told their children the stories of Moses and Aaron, and also of gracious Miriam (the Hebrew for 'Mary') who took a tambourine and led the women in dancing and singing,

'Sing to the Lord,
for he is highly exalted.
The horse and its rider
he has hurled into the seas'   (Exodus 15:21).

However, not all of the prophets were sincere. Some of those who purported to speak in the Lord's name were only prophesying for money. Two of the New Testament writers name false leaders in former times; just as there are still people who pretend to speak for God today, but they are not the Lord's mouthpieces. Peter speaks of those who 'have left the straight way and wandered off to follow the way of Balaam son of Beor, who loved the wages of wickedness' (2 Peter 2:15). And Jude takes up the same theme: 'Woe to them! They have taken the way of Cain; they have rushed for profit into Balaam's error; they have been destroyed in Korah's rebellion' (Jude 11).

The background to these stories concerns the time when Balak, King of Moab, was worried because the children of Israel were getting close to the promised land. He was anxious because he and the Midianites did not want Israel there, so he hired Balaam, son of Beor, to go and curse the Israelites. Balaam was a kind of prophet, yet when he opened his mouth to curse them only blessings upon Israel came out. (The full story is in Numbers 22–24.)

Thirdly, the Lord wanted Israel to remember the way in which he had led them through many difficulties. From the numerous incidents he could have cited, he chose the time when the children of Israel crossed over the River Jordan when it was in full flood. Shittim was the last place where the Israelites slept on the east of the Jordan, before they crossed it, and Gilgal was the first place where they set up camp after they had crossed the river.

These were all marvellous interventions of the Lord on behalf of his people and Micah's message was that God was wanting them to remember those salvation occurrences which had often happened in their past history.

After reminding the people of their deliverances, God, through his servant Micah, said something like this: 'This is my case. I have blessed you times without number and you have had absolutely no cause to treat me as you are. So, why do you keep sinning against me?'

These are things which we all need to consider today. All of us need to examine our hearts to see whether they are right with God. Periodically the Lord says to his own blood-bought people, 'Remember all I have done for you. Remember all the way I have led you and blessed you' (see Deuteronomy 8:2). We recall the Lord's greatest blessings for us every time we gather around the Lord's Table. We take the bread and wine in remembrance of him and in thanksgiving for the great salvation he has wrought for us.

Israel's answer (6:6–7)

The people of Israel wanted to know what they could do about their dreadful situation. They did not deny their sin, and they desired to do something to encourage God to forget their wrong-doing and forgive them. The problem for them was: how could they persuade the Lord to forgive them?

So they asked if they should bring the choicest of their possessions as sacrifices to the Lord. They knew that they should not approach the Lord empty-handed. They said, 'Shall I come before him with burnt offerings?' In a burnt offering the whole of the animal's carcass was burnt. This meant that in these cases there was no food left over for the people to eat. Everything was given to the Lord.

If that would not turn away God's anger from them, perhaps they should give calves which were a year old. These were those which had been carefully looked after for a whole year. Such calves were just coming into the prime of their usefulness; they would fetch a great deal of money in the markets. The people were saying, 'shall we offer these valuable things to the Lord in an attempt to get him to overlook our sins?'

Then, having spoken about quality, they started to wonder if quantity would pacify the Lord's anger. Their question was: 'Will the Lord be pleased with thousands of rams?' They would have known about those occasions when Solomon and other kings had gone to tremendous lengths and offered a great many animals as sacrifices to God (see 1 Kings 3:4; 8:63; 2 Chronicles 30:24; 35:7). If thousands of rams would not suffice, did God require them to offer 'ten thousand rivers of oil'? Oil was something which was associated with worship; oil was often offered with the Levitical sacrifices. However, neither of these two things was actually required by the law of the Lord.

Next the people suggested something which was quite terrible. They asked, 'Shall I offer my firstborn for my transgression, the fruit of my body for the sin of my soul?' So grieved were they about their sin that the heathen were even prepared to kill their most precious possession (their child) as an atonement for their sins. But God required none of these things. The Judeans should have known that child sacrifice was expressly forbidden by the Lord (Leviticus 18:21).

The people had many things to suggest, but each one of them was greeted with a resounding 'No'. So, after offering a number of things which might have turned away God's wrath at their sin, the people became silent. It seemed that they had nothing more to say. This does not, of course, mean that the people thought they could be saved because of their performances of works which pleased God. They were saved because God was faithful to his covenant promise that he would be their God and they would be his people. However, they knew that, despite their covenant relationship with God, their sin had created a barrier which was preventing them from coming to God with a clear conscience.

God's response (6:8)

After all of these suggestions Micah told the people what God actually required of them. In fact, he chided them because they already knew what they ought to do. The Lord said, 'He has showed you, O man, what is good.' By saying, 'O man,' he is speaking as though he is addressing each one individually. He often addresses nations in a personal way because of their sin.

The people wanted to know what they should do, so God said, 'What does the Lord require of you?' The Lord himself gives the answer, and it comes in three parts. Firstly, he said that they were to 'act justly'. This is the very thing that they were failing to do. Everyone was out for what they could get for themselves. They behaved as though justice was something which should be meted out by others, but not by them.

Secondly, they were to 'love mercy'. After all, God had been merciful to them so many times. He had taken pity upon them time after time when they did not deserve it. Therefore they, in turn, should be merciful to others.

Thirdly, they should 'walk humbly with [their] God'. This is a call which is often found in the Scriptures but so often the Judeans found it a difficult thing to do because they were far too proud. They were puffed up because they were God's chosen people, yet they had nothing to be proud of. They were not chosen by God because there was anything special about them. They were chosen simply because the Lord decided to have mercy upon them and show his love to them (see Deuteronomy 7:7). God required them to be like Enoch, who walked humbly with his God. It was by means of his humble life that he pleased God (Hebrews 11:5). The Lord required the same kind of spirit from his own people in the time of Micah and he still does in the days in which we are living.

The real problem for the Judeans was that they were failing to obey the Lord. They thought that by offering many sacrifices they would obtain God's forgiveness, when all the while the Lord was saying,

> 'Does the Lord delight in burnt offerings and sacrifices
> as much as in obeying the voice of the Lord?
> To obey is better than sacrifice
> and to heed is better than the fat of rams' (1 Samuel 15:22).

As individual members of churches we are still guilty of the same things today. We say, 'I will put myself out and go to church; then God will have mercy on my soul.' Or, 'I'll go to communion, and so guarantee my place in heaven.' But this is not God's way. He says,

> 'The sacrifices of God are a broken spirit;
> a broken and contrite heart,
> O God, you will not despise' (Psalm 51:17).

Before any Christian can begin to do anything to please God he or she must be obedient to the gospel of the Lord Jesus Christ.

Israel's punishment (6:9–16)

Again God is calling upon them to 'Listen'. His complaint is with Jerusalem, 'the city', and the whole of God's people, 'O wicked house' (6:10). He says that the punishment of the rod is going to come upon them. It is obvious that by speaking about the rod God is talking about punishment, and by this he means the captivity in Babylon. So he counsels them to 'heed the rod'. They were to realize that this punishment was coming upon them in order to refine them and teach them God's ways. They were also to realize that God was the one who had appointed this chastisement. It was no accident. It had all been ordained by the Lord. And because of that, it would turn out for their ultimate good.

God next refers to the specific sins of which the people were guilty. They had amassed riches to which they were not entitled. These were ill-gotten treasures because they had obtained them by using false measures when they weighed out goods for their customers. Their ephah measure was less than the standard size and their bag was full of false weights (6:11). But because they gave imperfect measure, God had weighed them and found them wanting (see Daniel 5:27).

Another thing to notice is that these rich men were also violent (6:12). They had roughly wrenched money away from the poor—money to which they had no right. And then they had tried to cover up their crimes by lying and speaking deceitfully.

In the face of all this God told the people what he was going to do to them. He informed them that their dishonest dealing would get them nowhere. He said that he had already begun to destroy them, to ruin them, because of their sins (6:13). They would have food to eat, but it would do them no good. They would fill up their storehouses, but they would find that they had saved nothing, because God would send the invading army to destroy it with their swords (6:14). They would not eat of the harvest which they had worked so hard to produce. They would pick and press the olives, but they would not be able to use the oil as sun-cream lotion on their skins. They would crush the grapes, but would not taste the wine which their efforts had produced (6:15).

Why would they not benefit from their own produce? It was because they would be ruined and their people would be mocked. On top of all of this they would discover that all the other nations would scorn and deride them (6:16).

So why would these things happen to them? It was because they 'observed the statues of Omri and all the practices of Ahab's house'. The main thing that we are told about Omri (a king of the northern kingdom) is that 'He did evil in the eyes of the Lord and sinned more than all those before him' (1 Kings 16:25). Ahab was his son who reigned after Omri's death. We read of him, 'Ahab ... did more evil in the eyes of the Lord than any of those before him' (1 Kings 16:30). We all know about Elijah's great clash with Ahab because he married wicked Queen Jezebel and encouraged the worship of the heathen Baals. Micah condemned Israel because 'The people exchanged the worship of God for the false baalism of Omri and his son Ahab.'[3] Rather man admitting that this heathen worship was wrong, the Judeans were following the tradition which had been set up by Omri and Ahab.

Our response to this chapter

We have no excuse for not knowing what we should do. God has graciously sent the Lord Jesus Christ to die for our sins so that we can be delivered from the slavery of our wrong-doing. He tells us that we cannot be saved merely by offering religious sacrifices, whether churchgoing or good works (even though these are vital Christian activities). The Scriptures teach that the only way to please God is by trusting in the Lord Jesus Christ alone for our salvation. Those who know the Lord as their Saviour are called upon to remember with love and gratitude the way in which God has saved us with an everlasting salvation.

However, God also requires of us certain behaviour. We should act justly. Instead of clamouring for our rights we should recognize what we owe to others, and then give them their due. We should love mercy. We should not respond to human weakness and brokenness with contempt, but with compassion that really cares.

Finally, we should walk (live our lives) humbly. We should renounce all arrogance, remembering our relationship of dependence and submission to God's holy will. 'Amos, in his prophecy, called for justice in the social order; Hosea emphasized mercy; Israel stressed holiness; and Micah blends all of these notes into a richer, fuller melody.'[4]

The effects of sin

Please read Micah 7:1–10

What kinds of people have the deepest sorrows in their lives? Is it those who have marriage difficulties? Or is it those who have money problems? The fear of unemployment or failing health can also cause much heartache for many. Many people become very depressed when they hear about the dreadful situations which are prevailing in many places in the world today.

But perhaps the people who are most distressed are those who care for loved ones who are going astray. Some who feel very low are parents who see their children drifting away from everything which is helpful and wholesome. When they think of the child they bore moving into a lifestyle which could easily lead to drug-taking, vile practices and crimes of every kind they must be beside themselves with anxiety.

Teachers, who do their best to encourage their pupils to take a keen interest in their studies, must feel very disheartened when they discover that their students have been wasting their time and their money by just hanging around the street corners, instead of doing their homework and engaging in other sensible activities.

Pastors too, who have a tender love for their people, grieve and even cry out in anguish when they see young believers (and even mature Christians) drifting away from the people of God and the teaching of his Word.

This is surely how Micah felt about God's people who were living in Judah, the ones for whom he had a special care.

Micah's anguish (7:1-6)

The prophet was greatly disappointed with the inhabitants of Judah. Their behaviour made him weep, just as we weep when a loved one starts to backslide away from the things of God.

Micah had observed the condition of the Judeans and he was very sad because of their state. Do we have spiritual insight enough to notice when certain people show signs of growing cold in their allegiance to Christ? They may not stop attending church, but there is about them a lack of zeal for the work of the gospel. They no longer get excited because of the blessings which the Lord showers upon his own and they seem to take everything for granted and behave as if all is going smoothly when it is not. When they are gently questioned about their lack of warmth for the things of God, they immediately begin to blame others, instead of admitting that the fault lies squarely on their own shoulders.

Micah was disappointed at the lack of spiritual fruit in the lives of God's people. He said, 'I am like one who gathers summer fruit at the gleaning of the vineyard.' Yet, when he went to find those choice grapes, or early figs, there were none for him to pick. All he found was leaves.

What did Micah mean when he said that there was no spiritual fruit among the people? He went on to explain: 'The godly have been swept from the land' (7:2). So what an awful place the southern kingdom must have been—to have so little godly influence left among the people! This is how Micah proceeds to describe the situation:

> 'The godly have been swept from the land;
> not one upright man remains.
> All men lie in wait to shed blood;
> each hunts his brother with a net.
> Both hands are skilled in doing evil;
> the ruler demands gifts,
> the judge accepts bribes,
> the powerful dictate what they desire—
> they all conspire together'   (7:2–3).

These words do not need any explanation. It is clear what they mean: the leaders of the people were thoroughly corrupt.

Then the prophet speaks about the best people in society. He said, 'The best of them is like a brier, the most upright worse than a thorn hedge' (7:4). He means that 'They are thorns in their neighbours' sides, pricking and hurting where they should be helping and loving.'[1] Moses warned the children of Israel, 'If you do not drive out the inhabitants of the land, those you allow to remain will become barbs in your eyes and thorns in your sides. They will give you trouble in the land where you will live' (Numbers 33:55). But Ezekiel talks about a coming time of blessing when, 'No longer will the people of Israel have malicious neighbours who are painful briers and sharp thorns' (Ezekiel 28:24). In the New Testament Paul writes to the Corinthians about the thorn in his flesh which, he said, was a messenger from Satan, to torment him (2 Corinthians 12:7).

Then Micah speaks of the judgement which God is going to bring upon the land. He says, 'The day of your watchmen has come, the day God visits you.' And he adds, 'Now is the time of their confusion' (7:4). He means that because of their sin, God is going to bring great punishment upon them.

This situation sounds bad enough to us, but there is worse to come. They will not be able to trust anyone. This reminds me of what it must have been like in Nazi-occupied places like France, Belgium or Crete during the Second World War. No member of the Allied forces who had escaped from prison camp knew whom he could depend upon. Soldiers on the run were constantly worried lest someone was going to betray them to the Germans. Although there were many brave men and women in all of these countries who risked their lives to feed, care for and protect those who were fighting for freedom, there were some among them who collaborated with the enemy. Those war years, in occupied Europe, were a time of great confusion for everyone.

In Micah's day the enemy was the invading Assyrian army which surrounded Jerusalem. We can imagine that everyone was uncertain who could be trusted. We can see that, in these conditions, neighbours, friends, family members and even wives and husbands could not be sure of anyone's loyalty. This is why Micah had to warn,

'Do not trust a neighbour;
put no confidence in a friend.
Even with her who lies in your embrace
be careful of your words'   (7:5).

In such circumstances, 'Intimacy is no guarantee to fidelity.'[2]

Many years later Jesus took up the sentiment of verse 6 to explain that the love which his people have for him should be even greater than the love that they have for their families. He said, 'I have come to turn "a man against his father, a daughter against her mother, a daughter-in-law against her mother-in-law—a man's enemies will be the members of his own household' (Matthew 10:35–36). The Lord did not mean that we should neglect our families (indeed he taught that we should do all that we can to care for them) but, when the choice has to be made between our loved ones and the Lord Jesus Christ, then Christians ought to follow the Lord whatever the cost. Many believers have had to face that test during the terrors of Communist and various totalitarian regimes. We ourselves do not know when any of us will be put through that trial, but we must be ready should a time of great tribulation come upon us when our enemies will be the members of our own household.

So how were the godly going to behave in the face of such difficult circumstances? First of all, Micah turned his eyes away from the things around him, and he looked to God. He knew that, even though the family unit was disintegrating, God remained as firm and stable as he always had been. Rather than despairing, the prophet said with confidence,

'But as for me, I watch in hope for the Lord,
I wait for God my Saviour;
my God will hear me'   (7:7).

Micah's faith in God was unshakeable. He knew that the Lord would never let him down. He had discovered that, even though he might fail God, the Lord would never forsake him. Although nothing made sense to him any more (as he saw leaders abdicating their responsibilities and society disintegrating), he did not sink into depression; instead he was driven into the arms of his almighty God. He was like the psalmist who said,

'For I hear the slander of many;
there is terror on every side;

they conspire against me
and plot to take my life.
But I trust in you, O Lord;
I say, "You are my God"'   (Psalm 31:13–14).

We can see, then, that God's Word tells us that things are not as black as we thought they were. We may feel that we have enemies on every side who are plotting against us, but the Lord is there, and he will hear our cry for help. We may feel that all our friends and family are forsaking us, but we can still wait upon God, our Saviour. We may think that our leaders, and those whom we look up to, have let us down very badly, but God, the supreme Lord of all the earth, is still there and we can put our hope in him, knowing that he will meet our deepest need.

Israel's confession (7:8–10)

The people did not try to minimize their waywardness. They frankly admitted that they had sinned against the Lord. Confession of sin is the first step on the road back to spiritual recovery. Yet it is the hardest thing for many to do. Israel said, 'I have fallen' (7:8); 'I sit in darkness' (7:8); 'I have sinned' (7:9). There are some people who find it very difficult to say, 'sorry'. They try to blame other people for the faults that they have committed. However, there is no hope for any of us unless we repent of our misdeeds. We must all say 'sorry' to God for our sins, and we must apologize to others also if we have wronged them. We must ask them to forgive us. But there is much, much more to spiritual repentance than merely saying 'Sorry'—even if we sincerely mean it.

We must realize that we have sinned against God, who is holy and who cannot look upon sin. The people of Judah said, 'I have sinned against the Lord' (7:9). When David committed adultery with Bathsheba he sinned against her and also against her husband, Uriah the Hittite. But even worse than that, David had sinned against the Lord God Almighty. This is why he prayed,

'Have mercy upon me, O God,
according to your unfailing love;
according to your great compassion
blot out my transgressions ...

For I know my transgressions,
and my sin is always before me.
Against you, you only, have I sinned
and done what is evil in your sight'   (Psalm 51:1, 3–4).

There is no doubt about it; God is angry about our sin. Israel said, 'I will bear the Lord's wrath.' God is a holy God; he cannot look upon sin, and he certainly cannot allow even one sin to enter heaven. If any sin could enter there it would cease to be heaven because it would not be absolutely holy. So we must accept that sin has to be punished and we have to suffer because of our sin. When we have hurt someone very badly we have the guilt of our actions weighing very heavily upon us. Yet none of the suffering which we may have to endure will ever wash away our sin from our hearts and consciences. It is only the death of God's Lamb, the Lord Jesus Christ, who died on the cross, which can make atonement for our guilt and wash away our sins.

But even though Christ has dealt with our sin there are still other people who will try to attack us because of our weaknesses and inadequacies. They will say, 'God hasn't really forgiven you.' Satan encourages our enemies to say this kind of thing often, but when we are new men and women in Christ, we can fight back with the spiritual armour and weapons that God has given to us (Ephesians 6:10–18; 2 Corinthians 10:4). We can say,

'Do not gloat over me, my enemy!
Though I have fallen, I will rise.

Though I sit in darkness,
the Lord will be my light'   (7:8).

We can join the psalmist in declaring, 'The Lord is my light and my salvation—whom shall I fear?' (Psalm 27:1).

The believer, whatever his condition, can speak with confidence. Though we may be down (as the people of Judah were to fall, and sit in the darkness of the Babylonian captivity) we can still have this assurance: 'He will bring me out into the light; I will see his righteousness' (7:9). Our enemies may well call out to us, 'Where is the Lord your God?' (7:10) but the last laugh will be with the Almighty, and with us. Our enemies will eventually see the deliverance of God's people and be covered with shame (7:10). One day we shall see the downfall of all those who are the enemies of God. They will be utterly defeated and 'trampled underfoot like mire in the streets' (7:10). The same theme is echoed in verses 16 and 17 of this chapter.

The point is that there is an enemy of souls, the devil, who is very active in these days in which we live; he always has been since the time he was cast out of heaven (Isaiah 14:12). Also the evil one has his agents all about us. They are busy attacking the people of the world, leading them into all kinds of filthy and corrupting practices. But they are busy, too, in seeking to lead astray the very people of God. They have many theologians in their power, and they encourage them to teach their students that there is no such person as Satan nor is there any eternal damnation for the unsaved. These false teachers influence weak believers and make them discontented with the jewels of the gospel, so that they seek satisfaction in writings other than the pure Word of God. Satan and his agents are busy everywhere, seeking to hinder the message of the gospel as God's people proclaim it day by day.

The reaction of God's people today

We should all seek to produce good fruit in our lives. May all that we do, say and think display the glories of Christ, so that others may see his beauty in us, and want to follow him too.

We should seek to be salt and light in the world today. Let us all do everything in our power to put into practice the teaching of God's Word, the Bible. Let us be 'blameless and pure, children of God without fault in a crooked and depraved generation [shining] like stars in the universe as [we] hold out the word of life' (Philippians 2:15–16). And may society be all the purer because we are trying to show the beauties of the Lord Jesus Christ wherever we go, and whatever we do.

We should seek to be those who are ever active in exposing the works of the evil one so that our neighbours and friends may shun him and all his evil works. And let us be those who watch in hope for the Lord, waiting for God our Saviour, knowing that he will always hear and answer our prayers as he brings us out into the glorious light of his truth.

Our pardoning God

Please read Micah 7:11-20

'Hope' is a word which summarizes the longings of people who are down, but have not yet reached the depths of utter despair.

The world, and Britain with it, has often been faced with dreadful times of hardship. Sometimes it is a failure of harvest which causes the trouble. At other times it is a deep recession which occurs and, as a result, many people lose their employment and status in society. However, in such circumstances, there is one thing which keeps people pressing onward: that is the dream that perhaps one day things will improve.

Believers in the Lord Jesus Christ have a more certain hope. They know that, however dark the day is in which they are living, there is definitely a time of prosperity awaiting them. They never give up hope that one day the bright morning star will arise (Revelation 22:16) and they will be brought out into the light, into a period of great blessing, peace and fruitfulness.

A positive message (7:11-13)

Micah spoke to the people of Judah of a coming time of restoration. He put his message in terms which they could understand as he told them about the broken walls of the city of Jerusalem. It must have surprised the people to hear Micah speaking about the walls in this way, because at that time the walls of Jerusalem were standing as strong and firm as they had been for many generations. But, since the beginning of Micah's ministry, he had been warning the people that their capital city would be demolished and a great deportation of the people would take place (see 2:3-4). These things would come to pass because of the aggressive ambitions of the Assyrians, but why would God allow his own people to suffer? It was not because events would take place which were beyond the Lord's control. Nor would this calamity arise because the Lord did not care what happened to Israel. This would come about because the Judeans had sinned, and continued to commit iniquity.

Yet, despite all the adversity which was going to descend upon Judah, Micah told the people that there was hope. He said something like this: 'Although you will have to suffer ignominy at the hands of the dreaded Assyrians, afterwards there will be a period of great revival.' It was for this reason that he told them, 'The day for building your walls will come.'

However, Micah did not merely tell them that things would return to the situation that had been existing prior to the Assyrian invasion. He spoke of much greater blessing coming upon the whole land. He said that the restoration would not just apply to Jerusalem, but Israel's land-borders would be extended as well. The nation of Israel (north and south) had for many years been confined to the narrow strip of land at the eastern end of the Mediterranean. 'But' said the prophet, 'the day for extending your boundaries [will come].'

This was good news indeed for the people. They must have been overjoyed as they heard the details of the enlargement of the possessions of Israel. The land would return to the size that it had been in the days of King Solomon (see 1 Kings 4:21). Israel was going to reach up the borders of their enemies' territory. Not only that, the border would go north-east to Assyria and south-west to Egypt. Furthermore, it would extend 'from sea to sea', which meant that it would reach from the Mediterranean in the west to the Persian Gulf in the east. To complete the picture Micah told the people that their territory would one day extend 'from mountain to mountain'. He meant that Israel would reach from the northern mountains of Lebanon to the mountains of Sinai in the southern Arabian desert.[1] Other prophets also told of these same glad tidings, but they had expressed them in different terms. As an example we can read in Isaiah of a glorious future age when 'The earth will be full of the knowledge of the Lord as the waters cover the sea' (Isaiah 11:9).

At the same time as defining the areas of the land which God's people would inhabit, Micah explained where the rest of the peoples of the earth would dwell. He said, 'The earth will become desolate because of its inhabitants, as the result of their deeds.' What were these deeds that would cause such devastation? They were the persistent indulgence in sin, the refusal to repent of that ungodly behaviour and the failure even to acknowledge the existence of God. Because of these, and many other iniquities, the Lord declared that the people of the earth would count as nothing. The effect of this is that the earth would be as though it was desolate and uninhabited, and those who were not members of God's Israel would be banished from the presence of the Lord for ever.

So what is Micah saying to us today through these verses? He is telling us that there is hope. Some seven hundred years after Micah spoke these words the Lord Jesus Christ, the hope of the world, came down to this earth to be the Saviour of all of his people. Through the coming one the blessings of Israel are going to extend to everyone who puts their trust in Christ as their Lord and their Saviour. They will become part of an expanding kingdom of God. For these believers there will be restoration of mind and soul as they are made God's new men and women in Christ.

Micah told the people that God had erected the walls of his love and protection around them. The implication of this is that the Lord is like a wall of fire around his loved ones. In Zechariah 2:4–5 we read about the people of God in the guise of a city— the holy city: ' "Jerusalem will be a city without walls because of the great number of men and livestock in it. And I myself will be a wall of fire around it," declares the Lord, "and I will be its glory within." ' In other words, God himself will protect his own people from all the assaults of their enemies and the Lord himself will extend the boundaries of his kingdom. Isaac Watts put it like this:

> Jesus shall reign where'er the sun
> Doth his successive journeys run:
> His kingdom stretch from shore to shore,
> Till moons shall wax and wane no more.[2]

But there will still remain some people who will place themselves beyond the boundaries of his kingdom. The consequence of that action is that if they continue living in this condition then one day they will be 'thrown outside, into the darkness, where there will be weeping and gnashing of teeth' (Matthew 8:12).

Should the fact that we, God's blood-bought people, are inside the kingdom of God's love make us feel smug, and tempt us to gloat over those who are outside of his salvation? No it should not. The fact that the Lord has shown his mercy to us should make us exert every effort to go out and tell everyone that we meet the good news that Jesus Christ has died to take away sin and sorrow and suffering. He has died to bring his own into the light of his glorious presence.

A time of prayer (7:14-17)
By the time we reach verse 14 it seems as if the message of the prophet was beginning to reach the hearts of the people. There we read that when they heard and understood what Micah was saying to them they started to pray. They cried out to God, 'Shepherd your people with your staff, the flock of your inheritance' (7:14). Using this well-known and well-loved figure, God's chosen people acknowledged that they needed the Lord to guide and protect them. They were almost admitting that they had wandered astray.

This picture of God as a Shepherd is frequently used in Scripture. In Micah 2:12 God had said to Israel,

'I will surely gather all of you, O Jacob;
I will surely bring together the remnant of Israel;
I will bring them together like sheep in a pen,
like a flock in its pasture;
the place will throng with people.'

The same picture is used in chapter 5:4. There the Messiah is spoken of as one who 'will stand and shepherd his flock in the strength of the Lord'. Now the people themselves were saying, 'We need you, the Lord our Shepherd, to care for, protect and guide us' (cf. Psalm 23).

Judah acknowledged that they belonged to the Lord. They

said, 'We are your inheritance,' just as the psalmist had said, 'The Lord will not reject his people; he will never forsake his inheritance' (Psalm 94:14).

The people then went on to describe their present situation and their future hope. They said that they lived by themselves in a forest. Anyone living in the land at that time would have known the importance of being separate from the world, with all its dangers and enticement to do evil. The Authorized Version of the Bible translates this verse, 'which dwell solitarily in the wood, in the midst of Carmel'. Mount Carmel was a wooded area on the coast which jutted out into the sea. Those who lived there would be separated from everyone else. Another word for 'separate' is 'holy'. No one can live a holy life who does not live a life entirely separated to God and his will.

This does not mean that God is calling his people to shut themselves away from everyone and everything as monks do. But it does mean that we should not live in a way which is indistinguishable from the world. There must be a mark of holiness in the lives of every believer—a mark which can be seen clearly by Christian and non-Christian alike! Holiness is our calling so we need to ask ourselves, 'Is that how I live my life?'

What was the hope of these people who were separate? It was that they would be taken over the Jordan to the rich, fertile lands of Bashan and Gilead, and be fed there. In former days Israel occupied that lush land, and the people were again looking forward to a time when they would be in possession of the riches of that area.

In the same way Christians should be eagerly looking forward to enjoying God's blessing in future days. Believers will not always be living with the trials and testing of this life. There is hope coming, a day when God's people will enjoy the presence and blessings of the Lord for ever. This thought is a very challenging one. Are we looking forward to that time when God's presence will be so very real?

Then the Lord God himself spoke. He reminded the people of the blessings of redemption. He said, 'As in the days when you came out of Egypt, I will show them my wonders' (7:15). As God had delivered the children of Israel from the stranglehold of Egypt, so he would once again save his people from the iniquity of this present evil world.

In this next section the scene changes to a description of the downfall of the enemies of God's people. Micah spoke in very graphic terms about the overthrow of the nations. He shows how complete will be the fall of their seemingly mighty enemy:

'Nations will see and be ashamed,
deprived of all their power.
They will lay their hands on their mouths [in horror]
and their ears will be deaf.'

They will not be able to take in the enormity of their downfall. These adversaries of God and his people would be humbled: 'They will lick dust like a snake.' As they kneel in obeisance to Israel they will be 'like creatures that crawl on the ground'. Snakes and all other reptiles were considered by the Jews as worthless as they slithered along in their evil, secret missions.

Then Micah gives further details of the destruction of the enemies of God's people. He said that they would be fearful. They, who had often caused trouble to God's people, are now going to be made to tremble themselves. 'They will turn in fear to the Lord our God.' They will not trust God because they will be scared of him and, at the end, they will recognize the mighty power of the Lord. Not only will they be frightened of the Almighty; they will even be afraid of little Israel because they will be terrified of the power of Israel's God.

But then we learn of a sudden change of mood.

Words of mercy (7:18–20)

This is the culmination, not just of this chapter, but of the whole book of Micah. These verses especially show how God is above all things. The question rings out: 'Who is a God like you?' And the answer comes back: 'No one.' God is supreme and unique. Many years beforehand Moses and Miriam sang,

> 'Who among the gods is like you, O Lord?
> Who is like you—
> majestic in holiness,
> awesome in glory,
> working wonders?'   (Exodus 15:11).

What is so different about our God? Unlike all other, so-called, deities, our God pardons sin and forgives transgression. This is one of the things that any serious reader of the Gospels notices about Jesus Christ: he often forgave people their sins (e.g. Mark 2:5). He is the same today. He still shows his wonderful mercy to sinners by forgiving them when they confess their sin, repent of it and turn in faith to him. He 'forgives the transgression of the remnant of his inheritance'. In other words, he forgives those who are faithful to him—those who trust in his name.

The Lord does not say that he forgives the rich people, or even the religious people. He declares that he forgives the remnant of his people, those who commit all of their ways to him and his care.

The forgiveness that the Lord gives is complete. He is not grudging in his forgiveness. He takes no pleasure in the death of sinners. In fact, his delight is in granting mercy to those who fear his name and who love him for who he is. When we believe in the Lord Jesus Christ he treads our sins underfoot and hurls all of our iniquities into the depths of the sea.

Matthew Henry comments: 'He casts them into the sea, not near the shore-side, where they may appear again next at low water, but into the depths of the sea, never to rise again.'[3] Just as the pursuing Egyptian army were drowned in the Red Sea, so God will dispose of our sins so that they will never return again. God not only forgives, but he forgets our sins. He never hurls them back into our faces. He never says, 'Do you remember how I forgave you when you sinned so grievously against me?' The psalmist said, 'As far as the east is from the west, so far has he removed our transgressions from us' (Psalm 103:12).

God is always true to his word. He keeps his promises. He swore to Abraham (Genesis 22:17) and to Jacob (Genesis 28:14) that he would make of them a great nation (see Luke 1:73). All true believers are included in this great nation of God (Romans 4; Gal 3:6-29; Hebrews 11:12). We are all God's children by faith, the same kind of faith that Abraham exercised when he believed God, even though God's promise of a son seemed an impossibility.

God has promised that all those who forsake their sin and turn to him in faith will be saved for all eternity. However, this can only come about because Jesus Christ, God's only Son, died on the cross to bring about our salvation. He died to atone for our sins. He died that we might know the pardon of God. That is why we can sing:

Great God of wonders, all thy ways
Are matchless, godlike and divine,
But the fair glories of thy grace
More godlike and unrivalled shine;

Who is a pardoning God like thee?
Or who has grace so rich and free?[4]

Nahum

10

The justice and mercy of God

Please read Nahum 1:1–8

We have now moved on some one hundred years from the time in which Micah's prophecy was delivered. Although there are some similarities, there is also a striking difference between these two books. Apart from the prophecy of Obadiah, Nahum is the only prophetic book which makes no mention of the sins of God's people; it is entirely taken up with the impending destruction of one of the most powerful of the Assyrian cities—Nineveh.

Nahum was written some time between the fall of the Egyptian city of Thebes (which Nahum mentions in chapter 3:8-10) and the destruction of this great city of Nineveh (the obliteration of which the prophet continuously refers to as imminent—e.g., 1:1; 3:14, 19). So we can see that the compiling of the book can be dated fairly accurately, without any dispute. History tells us that Thebes was wiped out in 663 BC and Nineveh was demolished some fifty-one years later in 612 BC.

123

Because Nineveh is spoken of throughout the whole of the book, it must have been standing during all the time covered by the prophecy. Therefore, Nahum must have prophesied some time after 663 BC and before 612 BC.

The prophecy of Nahum is unique in the sense that he tells us that he is writing a book (1:1). He is the only prophet to describe his oracle (or, rather, collection of oracles) as a book. This means that it was not necessarily the result of verbal preaching; perhaps what we have in our Bibles is something which was originally written as a pamphlet for circulation and discussion among the people.

We know nothing about Nahum except that he came from a place called Elkosh, which was probably a town lying somewhere south-west of Jerusalem. This means that it was very likely that he came from the same geographical area as the prophet Micah.[1] The name 'Nahum' means 'comfort' or 'consolation', and, although his book is taken up with the theme of the destruction of Judah's great enemy (which thought alone must have brought great comfort to God's people), there are many other matters in this prophecy which would also have given consolation to the Judeans.

At the time in which Nahum prophesied, Assyria was the one great power whose terrible influence was felt throughout the whole region. People were in fear of the Assyrians for hundreds of miles around. History tells us that they were extremely cruel, and those who want the gruesome details can read elsewhere about the awful torture they inflicted on their victims before they finally killed them. Naturally everyone was terrified of the Assyrians and their city of Nineveh was, to the Judeans, a symbol of extreme evil. No one wanted to get on the wrong side of these people. Because of their very wickedness, they despised everyone who feared the one true and living God.

People of every nation were afraid of the Assyrians. Everyone was hoping that the Almighty would do something to destroy them, and no one could really settle down to live peacefully all the time these 'savages' were causing such havoc throughout the Middle East.

However, God raised up Nahum to tell the inhabitants of Jerusalem and the surrounding areas that he was going to deal with those who threatened them. But, strangely enough, Nahum did not start his prophecy by describing the wickedness of the Ninevites (the Assyrians). Nor did he begin by referring to the unease of the people of Judah. His first recorded words were a description of God himself.

The character of God (1:2-3)

'The Lord is a jealous and avenging God' (1:2).

In these opening words Nahum used the covenant name for God. He reminded the people that the Lord is one who has an agreement with them. He is the gracious God who promises to protect and care for all those who put their trust in him, and he always keeps all the promises that he has made to his people.

The prophet said that God is a *jealous* God. We need to go back to the Ten Commandments to see what this phrase means. In Exodus 20:5 we read, 'You shall not bow down to [idols] or worship them; for I, the Lord your God, am a jealous God.' The Lord means that he will put up with no rivalry. Just as a husband will not allow any other man to share his wife in those intimate ways which belong to the marriage bond alone, so God will not permit his people to give any affection whatsoever to any other 'god', be it a pop star or a quest for materialism. If anything at all is allowed to come between God and one of his children, then the Lord will not overlook it. He will show his jealous anger against whoever, or whatever, seeks to win the affection of any of his beloved ones.

God has an exclusive claim upon each of his children. He demands that they refrain from sin and anything else which might bring his honour into disrepute. He has purchased them with the precious blood of Christ which was shed for them on Calvary's cross, and now they belong to him alone. Because of this God's people today must each do everything they can to maintain their deep love for the Lord. Sadly, some people do drift away from the Lord. Christ himself speaks about this when he writes to the angel of the church at Ephesus. There it is said that the church had forsaken their first love (Revelation 2:4). We, too, must make certain that our love for the Lord never begins to grow cold. Because the Lord is a jealous God, he will allow no rivals for the affection which should be given to him alone.

However, the inhabitants of Nineveh had sinned grievously against God. They had destroyed the northern kingdom and had taken away as captives a great many of its people. They had treated all of their captives with great contempt. Some of their actions were even more vile than the worst of the wicked deeds committed by the most terrible of Hitler's henchmen. And for many years the Assyrians had been threatening the southern kingdom of Judah. It was for these reasons, and many more, that the Lord showed another side of his nature. He told them he was going to display his *vengeance*. Three times Nahum mentions this word in the second verse of the opening chapter of his prophecy.

There is more to vengeance than merely fighting against an enemy. 'Vengeance is retaliatory punishment for wrong which has been done. The Ninevites had committed great evils. Now they were [going] to be repaid for those iniquitous acts by the one who had solemnly declared,

"It is mine to avenge; I will replay.
In due time their foot will slip;
their day of disaster is near
and their doom rushes upon them!"
                (see Deuteronomy 32:35 and cf. Romans 12:19)."[2]

How can anyone read this prophecy and still think of God merely as some kindly old gentleman, living up in the sky like a rather absent-minded Santa Claus who regards everyone as worthy of a generous Christmas present? Our God is not only a God of love (he is that); he is also a God of justice. He cannot countenance sin in any shape or form. There is no way that he can overlook it, or its consequences. Sin, and all those who perpetuate evil, must be dealt with severely. Nahum said, 'The Lord takes vengeance, and is filled with wrath' (1:2). Indeed the complete and utter destruction which was soon going to be lavished on the great city of Nineveh shows that God will not allow sin to remain unpunished.

But there is a third thing which Nahum tells us about the Lord; and here we begin to see yet another side to his character. He explains that 'The Lord is slow to anger' (1:3). He is not like those of us who flare up in indignation whenever something displeases us. God is not quick to lose his temper. Indeed, unlike us, he never does lose control of himself.

The apostle Peter tells us that God is 'patient ... not wanting anyone to perish' (2 Peter 3:10). But because God is slow to anger, that does not mean that he is weak, or ineffectual. The slowness of his anger is a sign of his loving care. However, eventually the facts must be faced. 'The Lord will not leave the guilty unpunished' (1:3). The city of Nineveh had responded to a call to repent some 150 years before Nahum wrote. This was when Jonah preached to them. Then, 'The Ninevites believed God. They declared a fast, and all of them, from the greatest to the least, put on sackcloth' (Jonah 3:5). However, by the time of Nahum they had obviously fallen back into their old ways again.

How can a people be so saddened by their sinful behaviour, and repent in such a way that 'God saw what they did and how they turned from their evil ways' (Jonah 3:10), and yet, later on, turn back to their sinning? Unfortunately we can sometimes see this today in the lives of certain people who profess to be saved, or who in fact may be truly converted, but then backslide away from the paths of God's Word.

There is surely a solemn message for all of God's people here. We must not be lulled to sleep, thinking that God is not concerned about our unfaithfulness to him. We must recognize that Nahum's words apply to us and our sins as well. Paul quotes many Old Testament passages in Romans 3:10-18:

> "There is no one righteous, not even one;
> there is no one who understands,
> no one who seeks God.
> All have turned away,
> they have together become worthless;
> there is no one who does good,
> not even one."
> "Their throats are open graves;
> their tongues practise deceit."
> "The poison of vipers is on their lips."
> "Their mouths are full of cursing and bitterness."
> "Their feet are swift to shed blood;
> ruin and misery mark their ways,
> and the way of peace they do not know."
> "There is no fear of God before their eyes."'

Nineveh had turned from the one true God, and so, in many ways has the church today. Their tongues practised deceit; so have ours. Their mouths were full of cursing and bitterness. Are ours any purer? Cannot it be said of our society in these days that there is 'no fear of God before their eyes'?[3] The character of God demands that justice be carried out.

The judgement of God (1:3–6)

God's judgement is universal. He created everything, and everything is under his control. Whirlwinds and storms may cause devastation on land and sea, yet the Lord is never caught out by these destructive forces. In fact the swirling clouds caused by upheavals in the air are used by Nahum as a description of the dust disturbed by the feet of the Lord as he hurries about his work of judgement. Sceptics may say, 'Why does the Lord allow such terrible natural powers to wreak such calamities upon the world?' God's people reply, 'We don't know the reason that these things occur, but we do know this: the Lord never makes mistakes. We can confidently affirm that there is certainly some purpose behind all of these awful events in nature.'

Nahum was using the power of God in nature as an illustration of the might of the Lord being unleashed against sin and all unrighteousness, and this happens throughout the whole earth. He referred to the drying up of the Red Sea and the Israelites' crossing of the Jordan when they entered the promised land (1:4). God showed his power then by destroying the enemies of his people and bringing the children of Israel into safety.

Lest the people become complacent, Nahum reminded them about the strong oaks of Bashan (see Isaiah 2:13). They also knew about the lovely fertile area of Carmel (see Song of Solomon 7:5) and they were aware of the majestic cedar trees of Lebanon (see Isaiah 35:2). However, all of these things, at the bidding of the Lord, could quickly wither and fade should he command them to do so (1:4; see Isaiah 33:9).

Even the seemingly eternal mountains, hills and earth will not remain undisturbed for ever. Volcanic eruptions and earthquakes do sometimes occur and these are not merely quirks of nature. The prophet reminds the Judeans, and each one of us, that 'The earth trembles at [God's] presence' (1:5). Everyone who dwells in the world is affected by God's power in nature. These forces are only small indications of the energy which will be unleashed when the Lord shows his anger against sin.

If the mountains quake before God, and the earth trembles at his presence, what mere mortal can stand against God's fierce indignation? Who can endure his wrath when it is poured out like fire? This is a question which Nahum shouts out at his readers; he wants them to consider the answer.

This book was first of all written for the inhabitants of Judah, even though its main subject is the destruction of the hated Assyrians. It would be no good for the inhabitants of Jerusalem to say, 'It served those Assyrians right. They have sinned very grievously against the Lord and his people and they deserve all the punishment they get.' This message was for God's own people.

After this cry of preparation for judgement upon sin the Lord then turns the searchlight of his Word upon his own people. He says, 'What about you?' Some years later Malachi was to put the same question: 'Who can endure the day of [the Lord's] coming? Who can stand when he appears?' (Malachi 3:2).

It is all very well for us to say that blatantly wicked people deserve to be punished by God, but what about us? Are we wholly devoted to the service of God? Are our hands always clean? When we read this prophecy we can see that Nahum is urging us all to give careful thought to our ways (cf. Haggai 1:5,

7) and make sure that we are right with God. Matthew Henry says, 'The eruption of subterranean fires is a faint resemblance of the fierceness of God's anger against sinners whose hearts are rocky.'[4] We all need to examine our hearts to see if they are hard towards God and his law.

The goodness of God (1:7-8)

God is not only a God of judgement. There is another side to his nature. He is also a God of mercy. In the midst of all this language about the vengeance of God upon his enemies, Nahum utters this wonderful statement: 'The Lord is good' (1:7). It is for this reason that we can have hope. We have all been born with a sinful nature, we live in a corrupt world and we find it difficult to know what pure goodness is. However, we can see genuine goodness in God, and only in him. Many times in the Bible we read the Lord described like this. In Psalm 25:7-8 we read,

'According to your love remember me,
for you are good, O Lord.
Good and upright is the Lord;
therefore he instructs sinners in his ways.'

There are other scriptures where we can find the same kind of sentiment but we see the goodness of God most clearly when we gaze at the life of the Lord Jesus Christ as recorded in the Gospels, and when we view him by faith.

However, God is not only good, he is a refuge for his people in times of trouble (1:7). We all have troubles in our lives, and sometimes we are so burdened by them that we do not know where to go for help. We can turn to our friends for assistance but sometimes the problem is beyond their ability to help us. We can go to a religious teacher, but he does not always seem to understand what we need—and sometimes he is far too busy to bother with people like us. However, we can always take our troubles to the Lord and, just as Israel of old found that the Lord was their help, we too can discover that he is our refuge in times of trouble. In the two world wars many people found the words of Psalm 46:1 a tremendous strength: 'God is our refuge and strength, an ever-present help in trouble.' And many can still testify today that God cares for them because they put their trust in him alone.

He does the exact opposite for his people from what he foretold for Nineveh. Judah will be comforted, not merely because the Lord is a refuge for them, but because he comforts and consoles them by making a complete end of the people of Nineveh, their oppressive enemy (1:8).

Some years after this prophecy was given there was a breach in part of Nineveh's great city wall. History tells us that it was caused by a tremendous flood (just as Nahum had prophesied in 1:8); and Israel was comforted by the knowledge that Nineveh was going to be destroyed. It must have been a source of great strength for them to know that God would obliterate Nineveh and pursue all her inhabitants until they disappeared into eternal darkness.

Our relationship to God

We all believe in God, but do we trust in him? That is the question. He will only be a refuge to those who commit the whole of their lives to his care. He demands a complete transformation within us before he will call any of us his children. Jesus described this change as being 'born again'. He said, 'I tell you the truth, no one can [even] see the kingdom of God unless he is born again' (John 3:3).

To receive this new life we have to turn our backs, in repentance, upon all of our past sinful life, and place our complete trust in the Lord Jesus Christ as our Saviour. We cannot experience the blessing of salvation unless we rest in the Lord. Those who have become new men and women in Christ, through repentance and faith alone, have the joy of knowing that whatever happens to them, 'The Lord is good,' and he is 'a refuge in times of trouble'. They know too that 'He cares for those who trust in him,' he utterly destroys all of their enemies and he grants them his peace.

11

Good news of deliverance

Please read Nahum 1:9–15

One of the puzzling things about being a Christian is the fact that we who trust in the Lord often have many troubles, while some who never even think about the claims of Christianity appear to have everything go smoothly for them. They are seldom ill. They have plenty of work, while many of the Lord's people are made redundant. They never give the impression that they are ever depressed about anything and all that they turn their hands to appears to prosper. The psalmists spoke about this kind of situation in Psalms 37 and 73 and other psalms.

The people of Judah in the seventh century BC must have felt as frustrated as we often do in our day, when they saw the advances that wicked men were making in their land. The invading Assyrians gave the impression that they were achieving one victory after another as they advanced through country after country. Every town which they attacked seemed to crumble before them. Their influence and power were such that there is no doubt that they were the major power throughout the Middle East at that time. Year after year oppressive Nineveh grew stronger and stronger. One scholar tells us, 'Bas reliefs of the assault of Lachish during [Sennacherib's] campaign, now in the British Museum, show large numbers of carefully positioned armies—archers, spearsmen, slingers and others—all supplied with ladders, battering rams, and other assault equipment.'[1]

Things had been very bad in Micah's day, but even though some one hundred years had passed since then, Judah was still threatened by powerful Assyria. This was the situation: on one hand, there was tiny Judah (only two tribes remaining of the twelve which had originally made up Israel); and on the other hand, there was mighty Assyria which had conquered many of the lands which lay all around Judah.

Whatever could God's people do? They had proved that Egypt could not be relied upon to help—indeed Assyria had destroyed many of the cities in that land. So where else could Judah go? She could turn to her God and seek instruction from the Lord, via the prophet Nahum.

Words of comfort (1:9–10)

In his prophecy Nahum tells us something about the people of Nineveh. He says, 'They plot against the Lord' (1:9). How were the Assyrians doing this? They were conspiring against God's people. Although the Judeans had behaved very badly, they were still God's people. The Lord had not cast them off, any more than he turns his back completely on any of his children. Even though they often neglect him, the Lord still stands by his own blood-bought ones. He loves them and cares for them, however foolish and wayward they have been.

Various of the leaders of the Assyrians had plotted evil against the Lord (see 1:11) but this is the message given to all who seek to work against God: 'Whatever they plot against the Lord, he will bring to an end' (1:9). No lasting success can ever come to those who are the enemies of God. No blessing can ever come upon any who do not acknowledge the Lord to be the one who is in supreme control of all things. In Psalm 2:1-2 we read about nations, peoples, kings and rulers who all oppose the Lord, but the end of such people is utter defeat:

> 'The One enthroned in heaven laughs [at their puny efforts];
> the Lord scoffs at them.
> Then he rebukes them in his anger
> and terrifies them in his wrath, saying,
> "I have installed my King
> on Zion, my holy hill"'   (Psalm 2:5-6).

God denounced the efforts of Nineveh. He declared that all their wicked ways would come to an end. This is something very definite. When we say, 'I've got to the end of my book,' we mean that there is no more to follow (not in that book, anyway). The end speaks of finality. It is in this sense that God often refers to the end of the wicked. They were going to be destroyed never to rise again. This is what was going to happen to Nineveh. It would come to an end. It would cease to exist. The Assyrians brought much trouble to God's people. In 701 BC they had captured Israel and Samaria, taking away captive the vast majority of the population of that northern part of the land. Everyone living in Jerusalem knew about these happenings. As Nahum wrote, they were all waiting and wondering when their turn would finally come.

But Nahum gave them some good news, He said, 'Trouble will not come [to Israel] a second time.' He meant that torment would not come again from these Assyrians. He could say this because he knew that it was in his plan that the whole Assyrian Empire would shortly be utterly destroyed.

The Assyrians were to find that the things they depended upon for their protection and their joy would backfire upon them. At this point Nahum introduced the subject of thorns (1:10). These often grew to make thick hedges; an invading army could shelter behind such a barrier. It would provide some protection for them from the spears and the arrows of their opponents. But, said the Lord, although the enemies of God's people think they are safe, before too long things are going to go badly wrong for them. They will discover that rather than providing protection for them, these same thorns will trap and entangle them.

Then Nahum used a picture of wine (1:10). In their celebrations of victory, no doubt, the Assyrians found pleasure in wine and other alcoholic beverages (which they would drink in great quantities). Yet this wine, which would appear to give them great happiness, would turn against the Ninevites. In their heavy drinking bouts they were going to discover that it deprived them of much of their power of discernment. It would turn out to be their enemy, rather than their friend. In 3:11 we read,

'You too will become drunk;
you will go into hiding
and seek refuge from the enemy.'

What a strong warning there is here for Christians to be careful in their use of alcoholic drink! If we want to keep a clear head (and why should not every child of God desire to do this?) then we should steer clear of any overindulgence in strong drink. For many people this will mean that they will have to stay away from it completely. The words of Proverbs 23:31–32 are very salutary:

'Do not gaze at wine when it is red,
  when it sparkles in the cup,
  when it goes down smoothly!
In the end it bites like a snake
  and poisons like a viper.'

Thirdly, God said that Nineveh would be 'consumed like dry
stubble' (1:10). This is the picture: these wicked people would
be so tangled up with thorns, and so drunk with wine, that God
would pick up the whole bundle of thorns (Ninevites as well)
and cast them into the fire. They are going to be completely
burnt, as useless stubble is consumed after the harvest has been
gathered. To use the wine imagery again, we could say, 'God is
going to pour out his cup of wrath against all of these wicked
people.'

Words of warning (1:11–14)
Nahum addressed Nineveh as the Lord made reference to the
wicked leaders of that city. He said,

'From you, O Nineveh, has one come forth
  who plots evil against the Lord
  and counsels wickedness'   (1:11).

We do not know exactly who is being referred to in this verse.
The Lord may have been speaking about the Assyrian king
Sennacherib who had besieged Jerusalem over a hundred years
before these events. The story of that king's lying, deceit and
wickedness is recorded in 2 Kings 18:13–19:36. However, this
verse may be referring to the Assyrian king Ashurbanipal (669–
627 BC), who was the last great Assyrian emperor. On the other
hand, it could allude to every wicked leader of that evil nation.

Then Nahum spoke of a command of God concerning
Nineveh (1:14). He said, 'You will have no descendants to bear
your name.' The Lord had highlighted a very shameful thing;

everyone wanted to perpetuate their dynasty in those days. It would have been especially important for such proud people as the Assyrians to preserve their nation. That is why they made statues and carvings (such as we can see in the British Museum and other places) and erected great buildings. They wanted future generations to know how powerful they had been. It was vital to their pride to be immortalized. In that way they considered that they were gaining eternal life. But, even though they did all of these things, God said that their nation would just fade away. They would have no descendants to bear their name. Their national life would cease completely.[2]

Even the religion of the Assyrians was going to come to an end. God affirmed, 'I will destroy the carved images and cast idols that are in the temple of your gods.' The implication of this was that everything that these wicked people relied upon for divine protection and guidance would be destroyed. However, God's people know that trust in anyone other than the one true and living God will prove to be false and ineffective.

We see, then, that the end of Nineveh was certain. The Lord said, 'I will prepare your grave.' How was God going to prepare the grave of the Ninevites? The way he achieved this is recorded in our history books. He used the Babylonians, the Medes and the Scythians to dig Nineveh's grave in 612 BC. We can read in Ezekiel 32:22–23 how this prophecy was fulfilled: 'Assyria is there with her whole army; she is surrounded by the graves of all her slain, all who have fallen by the sword. Their graves are in the depths of the pit and her army lies around her grave. All who had spread terror in the land of the living are slain, fallen by the sword' (Ezekiel 32:22–23).[3]

This complete destruction would come to pass because God pronounced Nineveh to be 'vile'. The word 'vile' means 'light', in the sense of being 'insubstantial'. It is the word 'Tekel', which was used in Daniel 5:27. There it meant, 'You have been weighed on the scales and found wanting.'[4]

It is still true today; destruction will ultimately come to all who put their trust in any defence other than the Lord God Almighty. All who seek joy in anyone, or anything, other than in the Lord will be sadly disillusioned. Everyone who plots evil against the Lord and counsels wickedness will be utterly destroyed.

Words of hope (1:12–13, 15)

Now Nahum returns to addressing Judah. In verse 12 he prefaces his words with: 'This is what the Lord says.' Although this is a characteristic phrase of Israel's prophets, it is only used here in Nahum. So, because the passage is introduced in this particular way, we should pay very close attention to what follows.

God said, 'Although they have allies and are numerous, they will be cut off and pass away' (1:12). Even though the Ninevites had made pacts with other nations, in their attempt to subdue God's people, they would not succeed. In fact he declared, 'They will be cut off and pass away.' Numbers do not concern the Lord. It is not those who appear to be full of strength who will win the victory. It is those who have the Lord on their side who will overcome. It is 'not by might nor by power, but by my Spirit, says the Lord Almighty' (Zechariah 4:6). Paul writes something very similar when he asks, 'If God is for us, who can be against us?' (Romans 8:31).

We may feel that life is one great battle. We may wonder how much longer we can last out against all the pressures of life. But the Lord himself tells us that although our enemies may seem to be very numerous and powerful, despite the fact that they appear to have persuaded many others to side with them against us, yet they will soon be cut off and pass away. God will bring them to an end (1:9), and they will end up in darkness (1:8).

Elijah felt very alone on Mount Carmel. He assumed that he was the only one who remained true to Israel's God. However, he discovered that there were 450 other people who had not bowed the knee to Baal. So when we feel that everyone has deserted us, we should remember that the Lord Jesus Christ said, 'surely I am with you always, to the very end of the age' (Matthew 28:20).

> 'So we say with confidence,
> "The Lord is my helper; I will not be afraid.
> What can man do to me?"'   (Hebrews 13:6).

Here in Nahum the Lord promised Judah that their punishment would come to an end (1:12). It was God himself who had caused his people to suffer for their sin of disobedience to himself and his law. But he told them that the agony would not go on for ever. They would still have to go through the exile in Babylon. However, there would be a time in the future when they would have to suffer no longer. The yoke of the oppression of their enemies (which had bound them fast) would be broken (1:13). In fact, God himself would take their shackles away. He did that when he sent his own dear Son, the Lord Jesus Christ, to die on the cross for them. Through Christ's death, everyone who trusts in him will discover that he is a refuge for them (cf. 1:7). To those who are true believers the Lord said, 'I will afflict you no more,' because all of their sins have been taken away by the death of Jesus on the cross.

Then Nahum almost breaks out with song in verse 15:

> 'Look, there on the mountains,
> the feet of one who brings good news,
> who proclaims peace!

Celebrate your festivals, O Judah,
and fulfil your vows.
No more will the wicked invade you;
they will be completely destroyed.'

The mountains spoken of here are the hills of Jerusalem and Judah. Nahum was exhorting the people to look up to those hills (cf. Psalm 121:1). One day before long they would see the swift-running feet of a messenger. The message he was going to bring was one of good news. He would tell them of peace for the whole of Judah. He would say that the enemy had been defeated. They would learn that the Assyrian threat had been removed and they would then be free to go and celebrate their religious feasts (Numbers 28-29). They could be sure that they would have no more trouble from their awful enemy.

Isaiah had used very similar words:

'How beautiful on the mountains
are the feet of those who bring good news,
who proclaim peace,
who bring good tidings,
who proclaim salvation,
who say to Zion, "Your God reigns!"'   (Isaiah 52:7).

The words in Nahum referred to the deliverance of the people from the Babylonian exile. That was good news indeed. It spoke of freedom for those who had been cut off from Jerusalem and restoration to their own people and their own land.

Finally, Paul takes up part of this same message in Romans 10:15 where he says, 'It is written, "How beautiful are the feet of those who bring good news!" ' Here the messenger is a preacher who brings good news, and this news is called 'the gospel' (meaning 'good news'). It tells of deliverance from sin through the victory won through the death of the Lord Jesus Christ. And these same blessings flowing from Christ's death are available for all who will come to him in repentance and faith.

12

The restoration of Israel

Please read Nahum 2:1–13

When I was a lad Hitler ruled over a large part of Europe, and other wicked powers, with whom the Nazis had alliances, had vast areas of the rest of this globe under their control. It seemed to me, at that time, that there could be no end to the misery that we all felt. Not only were there 'dog fights' going on in the skies over our heads (in the summer and autumn of 1940) and bombing raids at any time, but the cry which we often heard when we tried to buy particular commodities was, 'Don't you know there's a war on?' There seemed to be no hope of any deliverance from the pressures which we all felt. All I had ever been aware of was the wicked influences of evil powers who were then dominating much of the earth. I felt scared all the time.

The people of Judah must have felt the same kind of helplessness. For many years the Assyrians had been an oppressing influence on all of their thinking, which had affected every plan that they made. They could see no way out of their dilemma, nor was there any sign of an end to their troubles. Often they must have wondered whether the Lord had forsaken them, as things went from bad to worse. But then, with the advent of Nahum, God raised up a prophet who would give them great comfort—indeed that was what his name meant. As he gave them this message concerning the destruction of Nineveh, the great city of the Assyrians, they surely must have felt very consoled in their spirits.

We first read about Nineveh in Genesis 10:11. It is in that passage that the account of the founding of this city is described. Another part of the Scriptures where we can read considerable detail about Nineveh is the prophecy of Jonah. In Jonah 1:2 and 3:3 we are told about the importance and the size of this great city.[1] By the time Jonah was sent to Nineveh it had been a centre of wickedness for many years. However, after Jonah had preached in the city, the people had apparently changed their ways and repented of their sin. This was not what Jonah wanted to happen and, at the end of his prophecy, we have a glimpse of the Lord speaking to Jonah and pointing out to him that it was his prerogative to save a city, or destroy it. And, on this occasion God said, 'Should I not be concerned about that great city?' (Jonah 4:11).

Sadly it appears that the turning away from sin on the part of the people of Niniveh was short-lived, otherwise we would not read of Nahum telling the people of Israel that this great and powerful city would be utterly destroyed.

A warning to Nineveh (2:1)

The people of Nineveh were told that an attacker would advance against them. This attacker was, in reality, the Lord. God said that he would deal with all those who plotted evil against him and his people (see 1:11). Through Nahum God declared that he would completely obliterate the city so that it would never be built again (1:14). When Nahum prophesied time was getting short for Nineveh. The prophet said that the assailant would soon arrive. In fact the Lord spoke to Nineveh in unmistakable tones. At least twice he said, 'I am against you' (2:13; 3:5).

When the Lord states that he will do something, then he means that he will accomplish his purpose. This was no mere empty threat such as weak parents are prone to make to their 'little darlings'. The people of Nineveh had been given opportunity to repent, but their sorrow for sin had obviously not been permanent. Here, in Nahum, God spoke of the clear, unavoidable annihilation of this once great and proud city. We have already seen, when we were considering the second part of chapter 1 of Nahum, that God used the combined armies of the Babylonians, the Medes and the Scythians to carry out the destruction of Nineveh.

In an almost ironical tone the Lord called upon the Ninevites to defend themselves, even though it would do them no good. He used very strong verbs in this chapter—words like, 'guard,' 'watch,' 'brace,' and 'marshal all your strength'. The two words 'brace' and 'marshal' are the very same words rendered 'be strong and courageous' in Deuteronomy 31:6, 7, 23 and Joshua 1:6, 7, 9, 18; 10:25. It is as though God was saying, 'When I said to the Israelites, "Be strong and courageous," the secret behind their strength was I, myself, the almighty Lord. But when you, Nineveh, are exhorted to "Brace yourselves and marshal all your strength!" you only have your feeble gods to rely on. Whatever do you hope to achieve against such a God who is great in strength?'[2] What would be the source of their strength? It would have been the Assyrian lion, one of the symbols of Nineveh. However, when we read verse 11 of this chapter we discover what was going to happen to the lion of Nineveh!

Comfort for Judah (2:2)

It would have been a great comfort for Judah to have learned from Nahum's prophecy that the powerful city of their great enemy, Assyria, would shortly be destroyed. But that was not the only good news which the Lord gave to them; he imparted some even more positive tidings. He said that Israel was going to be restored. God spoke of Jacob and Israel in order to show that God's people would, one day, be rejuvenated. Not only that, he assured them that even the splendour of their nation would be revived.

What was 'the splendour of Israel'? The people would have understood God to have meant that the temple at Jerusalem would again be revitalized. What great joy it must have given to them to realize that Solomon's great temple, which once stood resplendent, flashing out its golden glory over the whole land, would once again be re-established! This must have been glorious news to the people of Judah. Over the years they had seen this symbol of God's presence beginning to fade and decay. Now, through his prophet, the Lord himself declared that the splendour of Israel would once again be seen in the land.

However, what these people did not know was that before these words of Nahum could be fulfilled their beloved temple would be completely laid waste by King Nebuchadnezzar and his invading army. The full meaning of the prophecy is that following this calamity in Jerusalem, after the coming captivity in Babylon, the house of God would again be rebuilt. We can read of the fulfilment of Nahum's words in the book of Haggai, but sadly the rebuilt temple never came up to the standard of its former glory (see Haggai 2:3). Even though the temple of Zerubbabel was rebuilt, and beautified by Herod the Great, it was finally destroyed by the Romans in AD 70.

Does this mean that Nahum's prophecy was only partly

fulfilled? Not at all. Today we can see something of the glory of Israel as we look at the redeemed people of God. That is where we see the splendour of the true temple of the living God. Paul wrote to the Corinthian believers, 'don't you know that you yourselves are God's temple and that God's Spirit lives in you? If anyone destroys God's temple, God will destroy him; for God's temple is sacred, and you are that temple' (1 Corinthians 3:16-17).

The destruction of Nineveh (2:3-10)

We have in these verses a highly graphic picture of the way in which the invading army captured the city of Nineveh. One of the striking things that stand out very vividly in verses 3 and 4 is the colour red. The shields of the soldiers are 'red'. The warriors themselves are clad in 'scarlet' and the flashes of the chariot wheels reflect the red glow of the sun, as they speed along to capture the city. The whole scene, viewed from a short distance away, would look like a sea of red flaming torches.

What is the significance of this red colour? We know that Babylonian soldiers wore red uniforms (Ezekiel 23:14) but it may be that the red on the shields of the attacking army spoken of here was the blood of their enemies.

Nahum proceeds to show us how the Ninevites went about their task of defending the city. It seems that they were totally unprepared for the attack—even though God had graciously warned them of it. We can learn from this incident how foolish it is of anyone to ignore the warnings which are written so clearly in God's Word. No doubt these Ninevites were thinking that no one could harm them all the while they stayed in their great, strong city. But they forgot that when the Lord is against a person, or a nation, then that person or nation is certain to be subdued.

Nahum described these defenders. Even though they were

hand-picked guards, they were not ready for what happened. As they ran to their places inside the wall, they fell over one another in their haste (2:5); then, halfway through verse 5 we are taken back to see the attackers at work once again. Nahum said they dashed to the city wall. They wanted to get there and erect their protective shield. This was to catch, and direct away from them, any boiling oil, or other defensive missile which might have been hurled down upon them.

As we are allowed to look down upon this scene we see that very soon, 'The river gates are thrown open and the palace collapses' (2:5). Ancient historians have told us that the reason the city fell was because a great flood broke down the city walls. This should not surprise us because it ties in exactly with what Nahum prophesied in chapter 1:8. There he spoke about an 'overwhelming flood'.

Next the prophet tells us about the effects of the capture of the city: 'It is decreed that the city be exiled and carried away' (2:7). Just as Assyria had captured many towns and taken their citizens away into exile, so the people of Nineveh would be treated in a similar manner.

For many years previous to this prophecy thousands of people had flooded into Nineveh and made it seem like a vast pool. But God declared that the glory of this pool was gradually dripping away (2:8). Kenneth Manley writes, 'With its inhabitants fleeing, Nineveh is likened to a great lake drained of all its water— reduced from magnificence to mud.'[3] There were attempts made to stop people streaming out of Nineveh, but even men the people were in such a hurry to get away from the turmoil that they refused to turn back.

Finally, we have a vivid description of what happened to all the glory of the great city. The word 'plunder' is used to indicate what the attackers did to the wealth of the city (2:8). Word-play is used to explain the effect of the attack. We read that 'She is pillaged, plundered, stripped!' (2:9). In the Hebrew language these are similar-sounding words which, used one after the other, build up in intensity.

Next we are given a description of how the people reacted to the attack upon them. The prophet said, 'Hearts melt, knees give way, bodies tremble, every face grows pale' (2:10). In other words, these people are frightened to death!

A summary of Nineveh's annihilation (2:11-13)

The strength of Nineveh was sometimes symbolized by lions. Often cities, or peoples, used the lion as their mascot. We read about 'the Lion of the tribe of Judah' (Revelation 5:5). In the beautiful city of Nafphion, in southern Greece, the lion was the symbol of its strength, grace and courage. In one part of the ancient city wall a carving of a lion can still be seen.

However, Nahum tells us that the lions' den of Nineveh would be destroyed. Verse 11 speaks of various stages in the development of lions: the full-grown lion, the young lion, the lioness and the cubs. Yet this whole family of the lions of Nineveh would soon be completely wiped out, according to Nahum. Just as lions go and hunt, strangle and kill their prey (2:12), so Nineveh had behaved in the same kind of way towards all the surrounding nations. But this lions' den would be completely obliterated.

Chapter 2 ends by giving a description of what the Lord was going to do to the Ninevites. He said, 'I will burn up your chariots in smoke' (2:13). Just as their chariots had flashed through the land with the speed of lightning (2:4), so now the lightning of the invaders would turn to fire and utterly burn all the defences of Nineveh.

The sword was going to kill all the young lions of Nineveh. Nahum was writing about the young fighting men of the once-proud city. They would be unable to prey upon anyone at all because they would be defeated and eradicated from the earth.

To make Nineveh's extinction complete Nahum declares that the voices of their messengers will no longer be heard. These same messengers had gone out all over the Assyrian empire, 'to command, compel submission, and extort tribute from her miserable subjugate nations'.[4] This would all come to an end. This kind of thing will happen no longer. No more will Judah be afflicted (1:12). Never again will these wicked people invade the land of God's people (1:15). Nahum triumphantly declares, 'God will make an end of Nineveh; he will pursue his foes into darkness' (1:8). All of this would happen because the Lord Almighty (the Lord of hosts) said to Nineveh, 'I am against you' (2:13).

There is a message here for us today. It may sometimes seem that everyone is working against us. We may feel in utter despair because of the strength and intensity of our enemies, yet we need to remember that the Lord has promised to restore the splendour of his people. Even though the enemy of souls, the devil, attacks God's people very severely at times, and has laid us waste and ruined our vines (from which we obtain all of our provisions), yet the Lord has promised to be a refuge for us in times of trouble (1:7).

It is not the enemy of God's people who will triumph in the end. It is the Lord who will win the victory. Sometimes he even uses ungodly people to bring about his purposes. In this instance he used the Babylonians to destroy wicked Nineveh. Some years later the Lord used Cyrus the Persian to overthrow wicked Babylon and allow the Jews to return to Jerusalem (Isaiah 44:28–45:1).

This is the message for us all. God will bless and strengthen his people, and overthrow their enemies. However, we need to trust in him. We need to lean hard upon him and commit all our ways to his cause.

In our natural state we cannot do any of these things, but with the Lord Jesus Christ we can even overcome the evil one. With the Lord, 'We are more than conquerors' (Romans 8:37).

13

The destruction of evil powers

Please read Nahum 3:1–19

The cry of the psalmist is often heard as, 'How long?' In Psalm 6 he cries,

'My soul is in anguish.
How long, O Lord, how long?
Turn; Lord, and deliver me' (Psalm 6:4–5).

In Psalm 13 his lament is:

'How long must I wrestle with my thoughts
and every day have sorrow in my heart?
How long will my enemy triumph over me?' (Psalm 13:2).

The same kind of agony is also expressed in Psalm 35:

'O Lord, how long will you look on?
Rescue my life from [the ungodly's] ravages,
my precious life from these lions' (Psalm 35:7).

The psalmist is concerned about the honour of the Lord as he pleads,

'How long will the enemy mock you, O God?
Will the foe revile your name for ever?'   (Psalm 74:10).

Then, when he recognizes the hand of the Lord in punishment upon him, he cries out for mercy:

'Relent, O Lord! How long will it be?
Have compassion on your servants'   (Psalm 90:13).

We can imagine the people living in Judah at the time of Nahum regularly thinking, 'Why doesn't God do something about these Assyrians? Why does he allow them to harass us all the time and cause us to tremble in fear because we don't know what they will do next?'

We, today, are tempted to think similar thoughts when we start to wonder how much longer is the Lord going to allow Satan to attack our church or our home. When we are being sorely tried we come to the point where we think of crying out, 'I can't put up with this any longer.' That is exactly how the people of Jerusalem probably felt in the days when Nahum ministered to them. Elijah was a prophet who experienced similar pressures. His prayer under the shade of a broom tree sums up the feeling when he sighs, 'I have had enough, Lord ... Take my life; I am no better than my ancestors' (1 Kings 19:4). However, God did not allow Elijah to give up, nor did he take his life from him. The Lord went on to use him mightily in his service.

So it will be with us. We need to remember that Satan is a defeated foe. He may appear to be very powerful and active in unsettling God's people, but it is Christ, not he, who has won the victory. When the Lord Jesus Christ suffered and died upon the cross of Calvary he defeated sin, the world and Satan. Believers should constantly keep before them this fact: Christ has won the victory. That is what this last chapter in Nahum is all about.

Woe is pronounced upon Nineveh (3:1–3)

Nineveh was a city of blood. The Assyrians who went out from that city shed very much innocent blood. Their desire was to conquer the world and they did not care who got hurt in the process. In these verses we have a very awful picture of their evil work as they conquered city after city. And all that there was left to show for their efforts were 'many casualties, piles of dead, bodies without number'; and the dead were piled so high that defenders and attackers alike were 'stumbling over the corpses' (3:3). These verses give an eyewitness account of a battle scene in those days. It sounds something like the script of a bloodthirsty film.

It is no wonder that the Lord pronounced 'woe' upon the people of Nineveh, because under his condemnation the Assyrians were as good as dead already.[1] We can see that the reason for this was because of the greed of the Ninevites. The King of Assyria (3:18) had set himself up as a dictator of the whole world. Yet what do we know about Sin-Shar-Ishkun, the man who was King of Assyria at that time? I do not think that anyone knows very much about him. He thought he was so great, but few details of himself or his activities have survived his passing. He is rather like the mythical Ozymandias in Shelley's poem of that name. The poem tells of a traveller from an antique land who describes a great broken statue which he had found half sunk in the desert sand. It had been buried for many centuries and was a total ruin. Even the head of the statue was shattered, leaving just part of a leering face. However, on the pedestal were written these words,

My name is Ozymandias, king of kings:
Look on my works, ye mighty, and despair!
Then the poet continues:
Nothing beside remains. Round the decay
Of that colossal wreck, boundless and bare
The lone and level sands stretch far away.[2]

Sin-Shar-Ishkun has been forgotten for well over two thousand years. We still remember dictators like Hitler, Franco and Stalin, but where are they now? Their power has been taken away from them, and they are all dead. They now exert little or no influence upon anyone. They considered themselves to be very great in their days, but they came to nothing in the end.

Nineveh was a prostitute (3:4–7)

Nahum now turns to a different figure as he compares the city of Nineveh to a woman of ill repute. Just as Nineveh's successor in evil work was called 'Babylon ... the mother of prostitutes' (Revelation 17:5), so Nineveh itself is likened by God to a harlot. The reason the Lord describes the city as a harlot is because the Assyrians had gone out and plundered the inhabitants of the surrounding areas. They had set out to enslave peoples—as a prostitute seeks to degrade others by her wantonness.

A prostitute's lack of morality attempts to lead men astray into unfaithfulness and evil behaviour—all for the sake of excitement. Not only that, it is at the expense of a man's marriage vows and his love for his family. Anyone tempted to consort with a prostitute should pay close attention to the instructions found in the book of Proverbs. There the wise man says,

'Now then, my sons, listen to me;
pay attention to what I say.
Do not let your heart turn to her ways

or stray into her paths.
Many are the victims she has brought down;
her slain are a mighty throng.
Her house is a highway to the grave,
leading down to the chambers of death'   (Proverbs 7:24-27).

One of the ways in which Nineveh led the nations astray was by using sorceries and witchcraft. This kind of activity was against the clear command of God (Deuteronomy 18:10). It is always a degrading thing to ignore the laws of the Lord. It is foolish, too, to become ensnared with evil practices which use unseen, demonic powers. Let us never dabble with witchcraft or any occult activity, and let us be very quick to dissuade others from becoming involved with this evil. We need to take great care with such things and never be tempted to think, 'Hallowe'en is just childish fun.' Consider very seriously what God says about these things.

The solemn truth is that the Lord is going to judge and punish all those who try to lead any of God's people astray. They will be brought to shame. '"I am against you," declares the Lord Almighty' (3:5).

Those who 'play the harlot' will discover that in the day of God's judgement their degrading nakedness will be paraded for all to see. David Baker comments, 'Because she [Nineveh], like a prostitute, had eagerly exposed her nakedness as part of her trade, so too it will be exposed to her shame before the surrounding nations.'[3]

Nahum tells us that because of Nineveh's sin, she will be like a prostitute who is forced to walk along the streets so that the population can throw filth at her. Nineveh will be treated with contempt, and just as an exposed prostitute suffers the humiliation of being treated like dirt, so proud Nineveh will one day be brought down to ruin; and when that day comes no one will mourn for her.

We can imagine something of how the people of Judah must have felt during all those years of humiliation at the hands of the citizens of Nineveh. But at last God has sent them a comforter in the person of his servant Nahum, the prophet whose very name meant 'comfort'.

Nineveh alone (3:8–19)

Everything that Nineveh relied upon would soon let her down. One of her conquests was Thebes, the great capital of Upper Egypt. Thebes spanned the River Nile and stood on the site now occupied respectively on the west and east banks by the twin towns of Kanak and Luxor, with the mighty Egyptian river forming deep moats all around it. The tomb of Tutankhaman was located very near to it. Some of the allies of Thebes were Cush (i.e. Upper Egypt) and Egypt (i.e. Lower Egypt); these were very strong countries. Two other supporters of Thebes were Put (no one knows quite where this area was) and Libya. Yet, for all her strength and that of her partners, Thebes was taken captive by the Assyrians. Her citizens were bundled away into exile. Her children were inhumanely slaughtered and her great men were led away bound in chains.

Consider these dreadful cruelties which Nineveh inflicted upon Thebes. God said, through his servant Nahum, that similar treatment would be meted out to the Assyrians. He puts it in these terms. He says, 'You too will become drunk' (3:11). He meant that Nineveh would drink from the cup of God's wrath. There was a day coming when the proud, powerful people of Nineveh, the conquerors of Thebes, would run away and try to hide from the anger God will unleash upon sinners.

The Lord went on to put his judgement in terms which they

would understand. He spoke of the defences of Nineveh and said that they would all fail. When the great time of testing came their strong fortresses would turn out to be so fragile that they would crumble away to nothing. Nineveh would be like fig-trees which are ready to be harvested. These first ripe fruits were much sought after. If people stood under the trees at the proper time they only had to open their mouths and shake the trunk. The result would be that the fruit would drop, easily and quickly, off the branches, straight into the waiting mouths of the eaters. What the prophet means by this is that the fortresses of Nineveh would offer no more resistance to the Lord than a fig-tree waiting to be harvested (3:12).

The Lord then points out the inadequacies of Nineveh's defence troops. He says that they are all women (3:13). He is not speaking in derogatory terms of the ladies; he is merely stating that those who would be left to attempt to defend the city would be women, who had not been trained to fight as soldiers. The question is, 'Where had the men gone?' The implication is that they had all run away in fright; they were cowards. However brave the women were, they would not be able to stop the outer defence gates of the city being forced open wide, or the wooden cross-beams, which held the gates shut, from being burned away.

Next the Lord paints a picture of the defenders hastily trying to repair the broken city walls (3:14). But it will all be to no avail; fire will destroy everyone and everything. History tells us that this is what actually happened. The city was completely destroyed and the Assyrian king died in the flames of his own palace.

Nahum then gives us a number of reasons why the city is going to collapse. First of all, he said that there was corruption among the traders. The merchants had multiplied like grasshoppers and locusts (rather like the way estate agents did in Britain during the house-buying boom years of the 1980s!). Yet these merchants were no asset to the city. Rather, they had stripped the land, until there was nothing left which was of any use. Just like locusts, these greedy merchants were going to take all that they could and then they were going to disappear as fast as locusts fly away when there is nothing else to gobble up (3:16).

Next the prophet told the people that it was not only the merchants who were like locusts; so, too, were the guards of the city. This is how he describes these guards:

'Your guards are like locusts,
your officials like swarms of locusts
that settle in the walls on a cold day—
but when the sun appears they fly away,
and no one knows where'   (3:17).

All the while everything is quiet the guards are sleepy, but as soon as things begin to hot up, and they are needed to defend the city, they move as fast as greased lightning, and they are gone.

Finally, the Lord addresses the king. He says, 'Your shepherds slumber' (3:18). The leaders of people are often described as shepherds in the Bible. In saying that 'Your shepherds slumber,' Nahum means either that the leaders are not awake to the seriousness of the situation, or they are sleeping the sleep of death. In any case by the time that the leaders become aware of the dire situation, if they ever do, the people will have left the city and fled to the mountains. The sad thing is that in that place there is no one to gather them and care for them.

Then comes the final awful word of judgement: 'Nothing can heal your wound; your injury is fatal.' They are going to die. This did indeed come true; Nineveh was utterly destroyed. Even the site of the city was lost for many centuries until it was uncovered as recently as the middle of the last century. What is there left to show of the glory that was Nineveh? There are just two large mounds of earth which are surrounded by crumbling walls.[4]

So why does God want the people of Judah to know all this detail about the fall of Nineveh? He wants them to know because it will bring joy to their hearts. They will clap their hands at the news of the fall of their bitter enemy and oppressor. She, who inflicted so much cruelty upon others, will finally herself be completely removed from this earth.

What does this mean for us?
God brought down Nineveh to show his righteous wrath against evil. He did so, 'to show that the most awesome, cruel regime imaginable was no match for the omnipotent God. To show categorically that evil in any form would be dealt with by a holy righteous God. Why did he assume our punishment and in Christ die for us? He wanted us to recognize our own evil. He wanted us to realize how we break his laws and abuse his holiness. He wanted us to go free.'[5]

With so much evil around about us, and in many countries in the world of our day, is it unchristlike to pray for the downfall of evil men? No, it is not. 'When innocent people in many lands suffer brutality it is a thoroughly Christian attitude to pray for and to take refuge in the soon-coming final vengeance of God on the wicked, and his vindication of the upright.'[6]

Yet, despite this prophecy being so full of the punishment of evildoers, there is much here in which the believer can take consolation. God's people can take great comfort from knowing that God is a just God who rules in righteousness. The government of God is strong and true, bringing honour to the name of the Lord and the blessings of justice upon the earth. When Abraham pleaded for Sodom he concluded, 'Will not the judge of all the earth do right?' (Genesis 18:25). God will bring about justice for his chosen ones, who cry out to him day and night (Luke 18:7). Believers do not gloat when they see the wicked being destroyed; they simply rest content, knowing that the Lord will take vengeance in his own way and at his own time (see Romans 12:19).

God is good, and he provides a refuge for his people when times of trouble come upon them. He cares for them (1:7). What wonderful words to find in the midst of so much talk of gloom and judgement! The Lord Jesus Christ said that he did not come to this earth to bring peace, but a sword (Matthew 10:34); he divides families when some are true followers of Christ and others reject him. One day he will come as Judge of all the universe. Yet this same Judge is also one who provides a refuge for those of his blood-bought people who come to him. To such he says, 'I will give you rest' (Matthew 11:28).

This prophecy of Nahum was fulfilled to the very letter. Just as the sentence of vengeance upon the ungodly was carried out to the last bitter dregs, so the blessings of the one who *is* the good news, and who *is* peace, are already being experienced even now by the redeemed people of God but they will be known and enjoyed in all their fulness in the glory days of eternity when every enemy shall be destroyed.

Notes

Preface

1. The refrain of Samuel Davies' great hymn, 'Great God of wonders, all thy ways are matchless, godlike, and divine', No.54 in *Hymns of Faith* (and also found in many other books, as are all the hymns quoted below).

Introduction

1. John Drane, *The Old Testament Story*, Lion, 1983, p. 123.

2. H. C. Mears, *What the Bible is all about*, Regal Books, 1953.

3. As above, p. 310.

4. William Hendriksen, *Survey of the Bible*, Evangelical Press, 1976, p. 250.

Chapter 1

1. Leslie Allen, *The Books of Joel, Obadiah, Jonah and Micah, The New International Commentary on the Old Testament*, William B. Eerdmans, 1976, p. 271.

2. *NIV Study Bible*, Hodder and Stoughton, 1987, p. 134.

Chapter 2

1. F. Davidson, et.al, *New Bible Dictionary*, IVP, 1953 pp. 402–3.

2.   Allen, *Joel, Obadiah, Jonah and Micah*, p. 280.

3.   J. Calvin, *The Minor Prophets*, A.P & A, Grand Rapids, U.S.A., p. 517.

4.   Quoted in Allen, *Joel, Obadiah, Jonah and Micah*, p. 280.

5.   *Hymns of Faith*, No. 309.

6.   Quoted in Homer Hailey, *A Commentary on the Minor Prophets*, Baker Book House, U.S.A., 1972, pp. 195-6.

7.   Allen, *Joel, Obadiah, Jonah and Micah*, p. 281.

8.   Stuart Briscoe, *Taking God Seriously*, Word Publishing, 1986, p. 91.

9.   *Hymns of Faith*, No. 294

Chapter 3

1.   Quoted in John Blanchard, *Gathered Gold*, Evangelical Press, 1984, p. 204.

2.   Calvin, *The Minor Prophets*, p. 521.

3.   Allen, *Joel, Obadiah, Jonah and Micah*, p. 297.

4.   As above, p. 302.

Chapter 4

1.   Allen, *Joel, Obadiah, Jonah and Micah*, p. 307.

2.   Peter Newall, *Bible Probe: Micah*, Anzea Books, 1981, p. 12.

3.   Matthew Henry, *Commentary on the Whole Bible in One Volume*, ed. Leslie F. Church, Marshall Morgan and Scott, 1960, p. 1151.

4.   Hailey, *Commentary on the Minor Prophets*, p. 203.

5.   See Allen, *Joel, Obadiah, Jonah and Micah*, pp. 317-18.

Chapter 5

1.   Albert Barnes, *Notes on Isaiah*, Knight and Son, London, 1852, p. 93.

2. Patrick Fairbairn, *The Interpretation of Prophecy*, Banner of Truth Trust, 1964, p. 196.

3. J. A. Motyer, *The Prophecy of Isaiah*, Inter-Varsity Press, 1993, p. 53.

4. Allen, *Joel, Obadiah, Jonah and Micah*, p. 327.

5. Newall, *Bible Probe: Micah*, p. 15.

6. Allen, *Joel, Obadiah, Jonah and Micah*, p. 330

7. As above, p. 336.

8. Wm R. Newell, *CSSM Chorus book*, Scripture Union, 1921, No. 135.

Chapter 6

1. F. C. Cook, *Ezekiel, Daniel and the Minor Prophets*, John Murray, 1881, p. 625.

2. Hailey, *Commentary on the Minor Prophets*, p. 210.

3. Derek Thomas, *God Delivers*, Evangelical Press, 1991, p. 392.

4. This is a verse from the hymn which starts, 'O for a closer walk with God.'

Chapter 7

1. Newall, *Bible Probe: Micah*, p. 24.

2. From Charles Wesley's hymn, 'And can it be'.

3. Hailey, *Commentary on the Minor Prophets*, p. 216.

4. Mariano Di Gangi, *Twelve Prophetic Voices*, Victor Books, U.S.A., 1985, p. 75.

Chapter 8

1. Allen, *Joel, Obadiah, Jonah and Micah*, p. 387.

2. As above, p. 388.

Chapter 9

1. See Allen, *Joel, Obadiah, Jonah and Micah*, p. 398.

2. *Hymns of Faith*, No. 233

3. Henry, *Commentary on the whole Bible*, p. 1157.

4. *Hymns of Faith*, No. 54

Chapter 10

1. See my comments on Micah 1:10-15 for more information about the other towns in that district.

2. James Montgomery Boice, *The Minor Prophets*, Zondervan, 1986, vol. 2, p. 60.

3. As above, p. 61.

4. Henry, *Commentary on the whole Bible*, p. 1158.

Chapter 11

1. Quoted in Boice, *The Minor Prophets*, p. 62.

2. Theo. Laetsch, *The Minor Prophets*, Concordia Publishing House, 1956, p. 300.

3. *NIV Study Bible*, p. 1358.

4. Boice, *The Minor Prophets*, p. 62.

Chapater 12

1. See *The New Bible Dictionary*, IVP, 1980, part 2, pp. 1089-92.

2. See John R. Kohlenberger III, *Jonah and Nahum*, Moody Press, 1984, p. 105.

3. Kenneth Manley, *Nahum and Habakkuk*, Anzea Books, Australia, 1980, p. 13.

4. Hailey, *Commentary on the Minor Prophets*, p. 264.

Chapter 13

1.   David W. Baker, *Nahum, Habakkuk and Zephaniah*, Tyndale Old Testament Commentaries, IVP, 1988, p. 36.

2.   From *The New Oxford Book of English Verse*, ed. Helen Gardner, Oxford University Press, 1973, p. 580.

3.   Baker, *Nahum, Habakkuk and Zephaniah*, p. 37.

4.   Di Gangi, *Twelve Prophetic Voices*, p. 81.

5.   Briscoe, *Taking God Seriously*, p. 116.

6.   J. Sidlow Baxter, *Explore the Book*, Marshall, Morgan and Scott, 1952, vol. 4, p. 204.